Long before a pandemic indelibly changed the world of education, Dr. Mekhitarian revolutionized blended learning PD across the state.

Now an entire nation of educators benefits from the roadmap laid out in this book that navigates the transition to in-person blended learning instruction. Both students and teachers will benefit from this robust plan that promotes thriving versus just surviving.

Dr. Silke Bradford
Senior Director,
Compton Unified School District

This work does not lament what is lost from our past, judge where we are right now, or warn of what is to come. Rather, Dr. Mekhitarian speaks to educators in all levels and puts action to practices necessary for high-quality blended learning with the goal of successful transition back into classrooms where lessons learned are not lost but leveraged to address issues of equity and access.

Jessica Conkle
Project Director lll,
Assessment & Accountability Unit,
Los Angeles County Office of Education

Dr. Mekhitarian is an educator with an uncompromising dedication to excellence. He has thought exhaustively through this transition we will all be making from Distance Learning to a "new normal" that heavily leverages technology.

Dr. Alyce Prentice
Area Superintendent,
Green Dot Public Schools

Mekhitarian's *Essential Blended Learning PD Planner* should be in the hands of every educator as we prepare to transition from a remote learning program to the post COVID classroom. School teams will be able to map out their site based plans to integrate instructional technology and blended learning strategies, while differentiated learning to ensure student success. This is the new must-read for every educator.

Narek Kassabian, Ed.D.
Principal,
Glendale Unified School District

INSIGHTFUL! Stepan Mekhitarian provides a clear path to an attainable future of high-quality education for all students. Classroom teachers will find insightful best practices, instructional leaders a nuanced approach to professional development, and academic institutions a must-read for teacher preparation courses. A perceptive, instructional guide for authentic student learning experiences.

Rebeca Andrade, Ed.D.
Superintendent,
Salinas City Elementary School District

Many educators transitioned from brick and mortar learning to distance learning overnight and are grappling with a future that looks very different from our past. Reading this book gave me confidence that our education systems and pedagogy in the near future will likely be more effective and equitable than anything we've strived for in the past.

Hrag Hamalian
Chief Executive Officer,
Bright Star Schools

This is a must-read for all educators facing a changing learning landscape. What jumps out at you is that Dr. Mekhitarian clearly knows what the inside of a classroom (in-person and virtual) looks like and truly gets that we all need tools we can use right away to make a difference for students, particularly those often left behind.

Dr. Drew Furedi
President and Chief Executive Officer,
Para Los Niños

We have entered a new world where now, more than ever, we need guidance to navigate the digital space with innovative practices guided by sound theory. Dr. Mekhitarian provides us with support for continuing our work with confidence, regardless of what the future holds. This is an invaluable resource for teachers, school leaders, and professors of education—and the stakeholders they support.

Dr. Elizabeth C. Reilly
Professor,
Loyola Marymount University

This is an invaluable resource for educational leaders and professional developers who are engaged in implementing effective classroom instructional practices that combine traditional classroom strategies with instructional technology tools. The author, an expert on blended learning and instructional technology, provides a guide with templates for schools and districts. A must-have resource.

Merle Price
Lecturer,
Principal Leadership Institute, Graduate School
of Education and Information Studies, UCLA

Mekhitarian's book is a guide and a pathway for all educators who plan to truly integrate technology in their classrooms once students and teachers get back in the building. The key now is to learn from the mistakes of 2020. This book has the lessons all educators need.

David Carr
Professional Services Manager,
Achieve 3000

Understanding the knowledge that distance learning provided, Dr. Mekhitarian creates a framework that shifts this information into the classroom where educators can expand and differentiate it for diverse populations. Offering a concise explanation of blended learning, content examples, and useful templates this book is a valuable professional development resource.

Stephanie A. Lowe
Teacher

In time for our present reckoning in schools, Mekhitarian provides a practical guide to conceptualize and actuate holistic blended learning at system and classroom levels. Based on successful implementation cases and research, this guide is quite useful for educators designing equity-centered technology integration, constructivist pedagogy, and effective professional development.

Dr. Ernesto Colín
Associate Professor of Teaching & Learning,
Loyola Marymount University

This book clearly articulates how blended learning can be used to enhance learning with visuals and ties to social justice that bring the ideas of the book to life. A must-have resource for any educator that is serious about transitioning back to the classroom and incorporating the benefits of a blended learning model that will inevitably improve student outcomes.

Dr. Silva S. Karayan
Professor Emeritus of Education,
California Lutheran University

Accelerating student outcomes requires addressing challenges head-on and generating innovative solutions. As we transition to a new platform for educating our students, Dr. Mekhitarian has provided a succinct blended learning PD plan for leveraging the best of distance and classroom learning. This is a must read for educators who want to ensure their students continue on the pathway to success.

Vivian Ekchian, Ed.D.
Superintendent,
Glendale Unified School District, Glendale, California

The COVID-19 pandemic is the biggest challenge that the current generations are living through. How we educate our students changed with a flip of a switch to blended/distance learning. If done right, blended learning is effective. Post pandemic education will very likely include blended learning as one of the options districts will offer. This is the book to get it done right.

Hagop Eulmessekian
Director,
Student Support Services Glendale Unified School District

The Essential Blended Learning PD Planner guides educators through a step-by-step approach to Blended Learning. Dr. Mekhitarian's methods have proven to be successful in our district and his suggestions are derived from actual experience, which ultimately provides a realistic and tangible approach for all educators.

Dr. Mary Mardirosian
Assistant Principal,
Glendale Unified School District

This is a fantastic resource and tool for all educational institutions! A clear and common-sense approach for implementing innovative blended learning environments that work across all learning platforms!

Dr. Lena Richter
Executive Director Educational Services,
San Marino USD

Dr. Mekhitarian has delivered a must-read for educators interested in guiding their districts or schools to an accurate blended learning approach. He explores instrumental ways of taking all we learned during distance learning and incorporating that into an integrated approach for the future. He has found the delicate balance of theory and practice to create a roadmap that educators can follow.

Dr. Matthew Horvath
Assistant Superintendent,
Personnel Services Beverly Hills Unified School District

As a teacher and instructional leader, this book is a call to action for all educators — a revitalizing approach that serves a guidebook for school leaders in a creating a plan that ultimately will reimagine the future of education.

Mary L. Tang
High School Teacher,
Instructional Leader

Mekhitarian provides school leaders with practical strategies for implementing a constructivist pedagogy into a blended learning environment. He shares specific guidelines for professional development and tech tips. This book is a valuable resource for educators to hone their skills as facilitators of learning and move toward giving students greater agency, ownership, and academic engagement.

Michelle Spencer
Founder,
CloverEducation.com

Dr. Mekhitarian addresses the shake-up that COVID-19 brought to education. He proves that there is no return to the norm. His shows that he has the expertise to explain what education will become. This book will guide educators as they move through these changes. Stepan shows change is a good thing and that we are on the cusp of some exciting times as education changes to be better for all.

Robert Martin
Director,
Product Operations Management,
ETS (Educational Testing Service)

Dr Mekhitarian offers a clear view of what effective teaching and learning must look like that's critical for 21st century learning, especially during this unprecedented time. This book is a must-read for administrators and teachers in providing differentiated support for our diverse students who come from different socioeconomic, racial, and cultural backgrounds.

Ruth Kim
Principal,
Los Angeles Unified School District

THE ESSENTIAL BLENDED LEARNING PD PLANNER

THE ESSENTIAL BLENDED LEARNING PD PLANNER

Where Classroom Practice Meets Distance Learning

Stepan Mekhitarian

Foreword by Michael Fullan

FOR INFORMATION:

Corwin

A SAGE Company

2455 Teller Road

Thousand Oaks, California 91320

(800) 233-9936

www.corwin.com

SAGE Publications Ltd.

1 Oliver's Yard

55 City Road

London EC1Y 1SP

United Kingdom

SAGE Publications India Pvt. Ltd.

B 1/I 1 Mohan Cooperative Industrial Area

Mathura Road, New Delhi 110 044

India

SAGE Publications Asia-Pacific Pte. Ltd.

18 Cross Street #10-10/11/12

China Square Central

Singapore 048423

Associate Editor: Eliza Erickson

Production Editor: Megha Negi

Copy Editor: Lana Todorovic-Arndt

Typesetter: C&M Digitals (P) Ltd.

Proofreader: Eleni Maria Georgiou

Indexer: Integra

Cover Designer: Lysa Becker

Marketing Manager: Margaret O'Connor

Printed in the United States of America

ISBN: 9781071843727

This book is printed on acid-free paper.

SUSTAINABLE FORESTRY INITIATIVE
Certified Chain of Custody
Promoting Sustainable Forestry
www.sfiprogram.org
SFI-01268

21 22 23 24 25 10 9 8 7 6 5 4 3 2 1

Contents

PART II: APPLYING PROFESSIONAL DEVELOPMENT STRATEGIES TO INSTRUCTIONAL PRACTICE   53

Visit the companion website at
http://resources.corwin.com/BlendedLearningPlanner
for downloadable resources.

• • • • Foreword • • • •

The Essential Blended Learning PD Planner is, indeed, the best of both worlds. It will help you take the best of distance learning and leverage it to enhance learning in the classroom. Mekhitarian is a wonderful, clear writer – succinct and to the point about a complex topic: **How will schools transition back to in-person learning?** How will they honor and leverage the skills they learned during distance learning as they rethink what the classroom looks like?

What I like most about this book is its comprehensiveness and clarity, and above all its focus amidst complexity. While Mekhitarian walks us through all key concepts in this transition, we remain focused on what is most important: how technology can promote constructivist learning in the classroom. Mekhitarian addresses the use of technology in classrooms with many techniques for ensuring that quality instruction is the driver. The focus is always on the learning. Around this core message of redesigning instruction, there are tools to help you and your team make every powerful connection and translate your learning to your context. Thus, we have "Professional Development," but always carefully in support of instruction. Ideas for implementation are evident, as is the role of culture and the role of assessment in the blended learning school. Particularly valuable is how social justice and equity are explicitly attended to every step of the way.

Throughout the book there are brief, targeted sections exploring Tech Tips, Blended Learning for Social Justice, Maximizing Technology for Learning, and how we can distinguish Distance Learning from Blended Learning. There is a technique to how Mekhitarian keeps the reader on track and cultivates deep learning (quality learning that sticks with you) while he addresses these key insights and practical strategies.

The Essential Blended Learning PD Planner is designed to help us answer these looming questions: How will schools transition back to the classroom after distance learning? How will we rethink professional development for blended learning? How can we embrace personalized assessment and feedback, create a blended learning culture, and bring it all together to make an actionable plan for our schools to move forward?

Stepan Mekhitarian takes an absolutely messy topic—major change under chaotic conditions—and makes it practical and clear. He does so succinctly and includes all important elements while always showing what elements need to remain front and center. It is a remarkable accomplishment. This book is amazingly timely and provides guidance for forging our way into a new future. Read this, and learn how we can leverage present possibilities to create a new world of learning for all students.

Michael Fullan,
Professor Emeritus, OISE/University of Toronto

Preface

Learning From the Sudden Shift to Distance Learning

In 2020, classroom instruction came to a grinding halt globally as the coronavirus disease (COVID-19) pandemic forced closures and pushed governments to institute shelter-in-place rules. With classrooms closed, students at home, and no timeline for when things would return to normalcy, districts had no choice but to quickly develop distance learning plans to ensure that student learning continued. For schools that could implement distance learning, plans and policies were rapidly written, online resources were compiled, hardware was distributed to families, and webinar trainings were provided to teachers as a crash course for online teaching. Almost overnight, many districts pushed learning out of the traditional classroom into the online space, regardless of the readiness or willingness of educators and stakeholders. Instructional technology vendors quickly made resources and opportunities for widespread collaboration available to districts, instructional leaders, and teachers to help navigate the transition. Departments of Education across the country looked for ways to support districts and facilitated opportunities to foster cooperation and share best practices. This sudden, seismic shift from traditional classroom instruction to 100% distance learning is only temporary; the day will come when students will return to the classroom and continue learning in-person. The traditional classroom, however, will never be the same.

There is no going back to normal, and that is a good thing. The distance learning experience exposed systemic issues that exist in the ways we approach education. What COVID-19 offered was a forced opportunity to tackle those issues. Distance learning ensured that our instructional practices were no longer confined to the four walls of a classroom. This sparked vulnerable but important conversations about pedagogy, grading, inclusion, equity, and much more. The groundwork laid during distance learning set the foundation for changes needed in our schools for a long time. Now, the tricky part is to transition back into our classrooms in a way that keeps these issues at the forefront and ensures that we continue to make progress.

· ·

There is no going back to normal, and that is a good thing.

· ·

This book examines how distance learning will impact the traditional classroom and how schools and districts can capitalize on this experience to enhance learning through a combination of effective classroom instruction and instructional technology. Most importantly, it will explore how these changes can impact equity and access for all students and reinforce the constructivist pedagogical philosophy and tools needed to finally close the achievement gap. The digital learning space offers unlimited access to resources, supports, and opportunities, and it is only limited by how educators and stakeholders use them; now is the time to take advantage of this momentous shift and forever alter the learning landscape.

Acknowledgments

I am eternally grateful to the people in my life who consistently supported and inspired me to give back to others. Writing this book would be impossible without the care and dedication of my parents, Vahe and Gretta, who instilled in me a love for learning from an early age. As immigrants fleeing a war-torn country, they emphasized that education in the United States would be the path to pursue my dreams, and I work every day to make that concept a reality for all students. I also want to thank my wife Lara whose steadfast encouragement and love helped me bring this book to life. I am also grateful to colleagues throughout my career in education who believed in me, challenged me to innovate and pursue opportunities to have a greater impact on student learning, and set an example for prioritizing students' success and well-being at all times. Their inspiration drives me to constantly push for new ways to advance student learning.

PUBLISHER'S ACKNOWLEDGMENTS

Corwin gratefully acknowledges the contributions of the following reviewers:

Jessica Baldwin
Teacher, Claxton High School

Ernesto Colín
Associate Professor, Loyola Marymount University

Hagop Eulmessekian
Director, Student Support Services, Glendale Unified School District

Bill Gallimore
Assistant Principal, Crescenta Valley High School

Hrag Hamalian
Executive Director of Brightstar Schools

Narek Kassabian
Principal, Wilson Middle School

Ruth Kim
Principal for Los Angeles Unified School District

Elizabeth C. Reilly
Chair & Professor, School of Education, Loyola Marymount University

About the Author

Dr. Stepan Mekhitarian serves as the Director of Innovation, Instruction, Assessment, and Accountability for Glendale Unified School District, and he was one of the main leaders responsible for transitioning the large district to distance learning in response to the COVID-19 pandemic. Stepan previously served as the Coordinator of Data and Blended Learning in Los Angeles Unified School District. He has been passionate about instructional technology and data-driven decision making since his first year as a public school teacher. He has a wide breadth of experience in classroom and leadership positions, and holds degrees from the University of California, Los Angeles, Harvard, and Loyola Marymount University (LMU). Stepan's doctoral research at LMU's Educational Leadership for Social Justice Program focused on the skills and training needed to effectively implement blended learning across schools and systems. He is a Google Certified Trainer, a Microsoft Innovative Educator, Blended Learning Universe Expert Advisor, and lecturer for the Instructional Technology for School Leaders course at LMU.

Introduction

When the COVID-19 pandemic forced schools to consider what teaching and learning would look like at home under unprecedented circumstances, districts across the world rushed to establish tools and strategies to transfer traditional classroom learning to a distance learning setting. I joined our district leadership team in its efforts to facilitate this transition and tapped into my background in instructional technology and blended learning to help develop a distance learning plan. Reflecting on the long-term outcome of this experience, I knew that teaching and learning would never return to exactly what they were before the pandemic. Instructional technology had been thrust upon many educators who were not trained in using it, and many strategies and tools that educators were apprehensive about before distance learning became part of daily instruction. Now that so many educators have developed capacity for using instructional technology, educational institutions—regardless of their size, location, and type—are all facing the same long game question: What will effective instruction look like once students return to the classroom?

To answer this question, I set out to write the book that can serve as a guide for schools and districts to reflect on their distance learning experience, develop a plan to incorporate takeaways from the experience, and effectively integrate them with traditional classroom practices to establish a robust, blended learning program for students and teachers. By combining the best of traditional classroom practices and instructional technology tools, we can create a powerful learning experience for students that fosters collaboration, constructivist and rigorous learning, innovation, and engagement. Most importantly, we can use instructional technology to close the achievement gap instead of widening it.

This book breaks down the development process into three parts, beginning with a theoretical exploration of blended learning and then moving to practical strategies. The conclusion of the book brings together the theory and practice from the previous sections and consolidates them into one cohesive plan ready for implementation.

- Part I guides teams through a reflection process about the distance learning experience and the elements that can inform a blended learning program, describing the components of a comprehensive professional development (PD) plan to prepare teachers for instructional technology use in the classroom.

- Part II applies the PD components to three main areas in which teachers will need support: effective instructional practice, formative assessment and data analysis, and a classroom environment and culture conducive to rigorous learning using instructional technology.

- Part III takes the PD topics discussed in the first two parts and guides teams through the process of bringing them together into one cohesive training and implementation program.

FIGURE 0.1 ● The Book's Framework

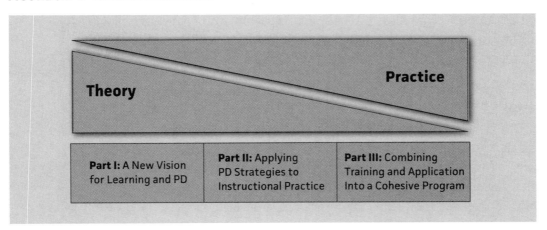

The beginning of each chapter includes a PD planning process flowchart presented in Figure 0.2, which shows each chapter's contribution to the journey from theory to practice.

This book is designed to be read as a team with instructional leaders at all levels: teacher leaders and school and district administrators. Working collaboratively from the outset

FIGURE 0.2 ● Blended Learning Program Professional Development Planning Process

Part I: **A New Vision for Learning and Professional Development**

Chapter 1: **Elements of an Effective Blended Learning Classroom**

- Effective instructional practices from distance learning
- Effective instructional practices from the traditional classroom
- A focus on conceptual understanding and constructivist learning

Which come from...

Chapter 2: **Planning an Effective PD Program**

- Peer observations in BL classrooms *(tips in Chapters 3 & 5)*
- PLCs focused on best practices *(tips in Chapters 3 & 4)*
- Tech integration with a focus on instruction *(tips in Chapters 3 & 4)*
- Research on BL theory and effective practices *(tips in Chapters 4 & 5)*
- Analysis of effective models in a BL classroom *(tips in Chapter 5)*
- Teacher workload sustainability *(tips in Chapter 5)*

That focuses on...

Part II: **Applying PD Strategies to Instructional Practice**

CH. 3: RIGOROUS LEARNING FOR ALL	*CH. 4:* PERSONALIZED ASSESSMENT & FEEDBACK	*CH. 5:* CLASSROOM CULTURE
• Differentiation for equitable access • Constructivist learning opportunities • Effective questioning • Student collaboration	• Assessments to gather actionable data • Actionable feedback for all students • Facilitating self-monitoring • Peer feedback	• Digital citizenship training • Learning environments in a BL model • A collaborative learning culture • Tech integration and management

And leads to...

Part III: **Bringing Training and Application Together in One Cohesive Program**

Conclusion: Bringing It All Together

- Creating a vision based on key takeaways
- Focused leadership during the transition
- Building your professional development team
- Collaborating with students and parents as stakeholders
- Soliciting feedback on distance learning
- Sharing blended learning impact on student learning
- Preparing students for a new world

brings multiple stakeholder perspectives to the discussion and facilitates buy-in to maximize the implementation opportunities. As you begin reading this book, think about educators who can serve as thought partners and invite them to join you in this journey.

Throughout the chapters, you will find several recurring features designed to start discussions, inform planning, and facilitate application:

- **Figures** show how various elements of the program connect and inform each other.

- **Fill-in Templates** pose questions to the team to foster critical thinking and reflection. These templates are available for download on the companion website.

- **Tech Tips** provide specific examples of how to use a tech tool to aid in the implementation of a concept described in that section.

- **Blended Learning for Social Justice** sections show how instructional technology can help close the achievement gap through differentiation and reaching students with different learning modalities

- **Ideas for Professional Development Sessions** give PD and instructional leaders ideas for sharing strategies and topics discussed in this book with their faculty teams.

- **Distance Vs. Blended Learning** sections help educators transition various implementation strategies from distance learning to blended learning environments, highlighting the similarities and differences in the implementation of various learning opportunities to guide readers through the transition from distance to blended learning environments.

The return to the classroom after distance learning has never been experienced on a systemic scale and will surely raise more questions. I am hopeful that this book will facilitate critical discussions about learning and provide applicable next steps to help educators find the silver lining during a time of immense uncertainty and create amazing learning experiences for all students.

A New Vision for Learning and Professional Development

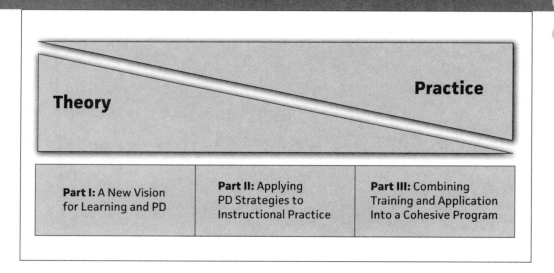

Part I: A New Vision for Learning and PD	**Part II:** Applying PD Strategies to Instructional Practice	**Part III:** Combining Training and Application Into a Cohesive Program

● ● ● ● ● ● ● ● ● ● ● ● ● ● ● ● ● ●

How Will Schools Transition Back to the Classroom?

This chapter will explore the successes and challenges of the distance learning experience and connect them to effective blended learning models that utilize a collaborative and constructivist—or meaning-making—learning approach. This connection will offer an opportunity to review your organization's vision for learning, develop a robust training and support program, and apply it to different elements of effective instruction.

LEVERAGING BEST PRACTICES FROM THE DISTANCE LEARNING EXPERIENCE

As students return to the classroom, educators will lead the transition from distance learning back to in-person instruction. This is a critical opportunity to take advantage of the lessons learned from distance learning and implement instructional technology in the classroom using a blended learning model—an education program in which a student learns partly through online delivery of content and instruction with partial control over time, place, path, or pace (Knewton Blended Learning Infographic, 2014). Historically, distance learning has shown varying levels of effectiveness in terms of student success. However, critically exploring its instructional methodology and applying elements to a traditional classroom setting can result in great learning gains (Harris-Packer & Ségol, 2015).

Part I: A New Vision for Learning and Professional Development

Chapter 1: Elements of an Effective Blended Learning Classroom

- Effective instructional practices from distance learning
- Effective instructional practices from the traditional classroom
- A focus on conceptual understanding and constructivist learning

Which come from...

Chapter 2: Planning an Effective PD Program

- Peer observations in BL classrooms *(tips in Chapters 3 & 5)*
- PLCs focused on best practices *(tips in Chapters 3 & 4)*
- Tech integration with a focus on instruction *(tips in Chapters 3 & 4)*
- Research on BL theory and effective practices *(tips in Chapters 4 & 5)*
- Analysis of effective models in a BL classroom *(tips in Chapter 5)*
- Teacher workload sustainability *(tips in Chapter 5)*

That focuses on...

Part II: Applying PD Strategies to Instructional Practice

CH. 3: RIGOROUS LEARNING FOR ALL	**CH. 4: PERSONALIZED ASSESSMENT & FEEDBACK**	**CH. 5: CLASSROOM CULTURE**
• Differentiation for equitable access • Constructivist learning opportunities • Effective questioning • Student collaboration	• Assessments to gather actionable data • Actionable feedback for all students • Facilitating self-monitoring • Peer feedback	• Digital citizenship training • Learning environments in a BL model • A collaborative learning culture • Tech integration and management

And leads to...

Part III: Bringing Training and Application Together in One Cohesive Program

Conclusion: Bringing It All Together

- Creating a vision based on key takeaways
- Focused leadership during the transition
- Building your professional development team
- Collaborating with students and parents as stakeholders
- Soliciting feedback on distance learning
- Sharing blended learning impact on student learning
- Preparing students for a new world

The dramatic shift to distance learning rapidly introduced instructional technology to millions of educators, but determining how technology should be utilized to enhance learning is a skill that educators need to master to effectively implement blended learning. Many educators were able to seamlessly adapt their instruction to the online space while others, who adopted instructional technology for the first time during COVID-19, did not have the extensive professional development (PD) support to learn how to leverage technology for learning in effective ways. There are several instructional practices that must always be considered when designing a learning experience, whether in a distance learning environment or the traditional classroom:

- Differentiated supports for equitable access
- Actionable feedback to students
- Effective questioning to facilitate constructivist learning
- Student collaboration
- Assessments to gather actionable data
- Highly rigorous learning opportunities

Effective instructional practices that promote these key features of high-quality learning look different in traditional and online classrooms. Figure 1.1 demonstrates how to dramatically impact student success by taking the best of both worlds—our most effective classroom strategies and online strategies—to create a blended learning program that supports all learners.

FIGURE 1.1 ● Elements of an Effective Blended Learning Classroom

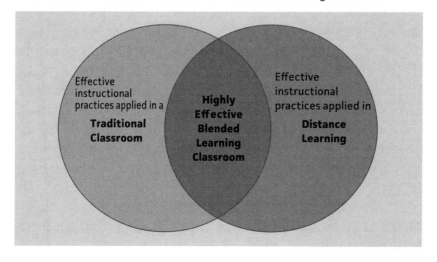

Determining *what* to incorporate in the blended learning classroom and *how* to do it are at the core of the transition. Establish a professional development task force comprised of instructional leaders at your school. Start with a collaborative analysis of successes during distance learning, and compare findings to pedagogical practices before the transition. Use Figure 1.2 to facilitate a conversation with faculty members and instructional leaders to identify how instructional practices differed during distance learning. Identify the instructional practices enhanced by the distance learning experience and the evidence that validates these claims. Be sure to solicit feedback from students to build their capacity as insightful learners, as well as to get their perspective on strategies and resources that helped them learn during distance learning (more information on resources to gather this information can be found in the conclusion). Use these findings and the Figure 1.2 to create a list of practices that can be enhanced by instructional technology in a blended learning classroom for PD planning. These practices will form the basis of the PD program we explore later.

. . . .

Be sure to solicit feedback from students as well to get their perspective on strategies and resources that helped them learn during distance learning.

. . . .

As you review your findings in Figure 1.2 on page 11. look to see if the practices you list are online versions of traditional classroom practices or if they utilize instructional technology to enhance rigor and promote meaning-making and discovery. Online versions of traditional classroom practices simply emulate traditional classroom teaching online. In these cases, technology serves as a vessel to convey information in the same way it would be delivered in a traditional classroom setting. In a true blended learning model, classroom practices and norms shift to facilitate student discovery. Figure 1.3 demonstrates examples of each approach to online learning. The more robust approaches to blended learning in Figure 1.3 show how a teacher can advance learning by using technology to develop activities that facilitate discovery based on constructivist learning. Work with your task force to fill out your own examples in Figure 1.3. This will help you develop a common understanding of the kinds of rich learning experiences instructional technology can facilitate.

FIGURE 1.2 ● Determining What Distance Learning Practices to Incorporate in Your Blended Learning Program

INSTRUCTIONAL PRACTICE	IMPLEMENTATION DURING TRADITIONAL CLASSROOM INSTRUCTION	IMPLEMENTATION DURING DISTANCE LEARNING	WAYS DISTANCE INSTRUCTION ENHANCED LEARNING	EVIDENCE OF EFFECTIVENESS	POTENTIAL IMPACT IN A BLENDED LEARNING CLASSROOM
Differentiated supports for equitable access					
Actionable feedback to students					
Effective questioning to facilitate constructivist learning					
Student collaboration					
Assessments to gather actionable data					
Highly rigorous learning opportunities					

Figure I.2 is available as a downloadable template on the Companion Website at Resources.Corwin.com/BlendedLearningPlanner.

FIGURE 1.3 ● Maximizing Technology for Learning

	ONLINE VERSIONS OF TRADITIONAL CLASSROOM PRACTICES	UTILIZE INSTRUCTIONAL TECHNOLOGY TO ENHANCE RIGOR AND PROMOTE MEANING-MAKING AND DISCOVERY
Math Example	The teacher records a screencast introducing the Pythagorean Theorem and explaining how it can be used to calculate the hypotenuse of a right triangle. The teacher then assigns several problems with figures of right triangles and asks students to calculate the hypotenuse for each one.	The teacher poses a question involving a quadrilateral backyard and provides rigorous prompts to facilitate discussion and online research, ultimately leading to students deriving the Pythagorean Theorem, developing an adjustable model, and applying it to solve the initial problem.
Social Science Example	The teacher directs students to an article and an online documentary film about important historical figures during the American Revolution and asks students to select one figure and write a short paper about their contribution. Students are expected to conduct their own research and include it in the paper.	The teacher asks students to research and identify several key factors that contributed to the outcome of the American Revolution. Students choose one figure from each side and prepare a short paper explaining the impact of that person. Then, student groups combine their summaries in an online, interactive format and share with the rest of the class. This can include video presentations, interactive maps, and virtual interviews with experts on the subject. Based on the group projects, students vote on the impactful figure and justify their selection.
Your example:		
Your example:		
Your example:		

 Figure 1.3 is available as a downloadable template on the Companion Website at Resources.Corwin.com/BlendedLearningPlanner.

WHAT IS BLENDED LEARNING?

To maximize the instructional impact of blended learning, we must understand the potential of instructional technology and its role in the classroom. Instructional technology can dramatically impact all students' learning if educators are trained to implement it effectively (Pregot, 2013). Blended learning revolutionizes the traditional relationship between teachers, students, and content by shifting the roles of all three in the classroom. In a traditional classroom, the teacher's role has been to share content knowledge directly with students. In the blended learning classroom, students drive the learning process through discovery and by exploring content and how it builds on their previous knowledge. This also builds students' capacity for self-monitoring and independence, both critical levers of culturally responsive learning.

· ·

The distance learning experience rapidly expanded technical proficiency, but to truly move toward a blended learning model—whether in an online or classroom setting—we must develop instructional practices to promote the meaning-making and differentiated approach.

· ·

The role of the teacher is to support and carefully facilitate this student-driven learning experience. Blended learning includes many of the characteristics of effective learning approaches praised by educators and researchers—differentiated, self-paced, discovery based, and collaborative—but utilizes technology to facilitate these types of learning. Research by Milthorpe et al. (2018) confirms "many of the narratives about blended learning ... in terms of increased student engagement, access, interactivity, and flexibility" (p. 357).

In the past, limitations in technology, pedagogical research, and reluctance to engage with technology have impacted the effectiveness and scope of this type of instruction. The distance learning experience rapidly expanded technical proficiency, but to truly move toward a blended learning model—whether in an online or classroom setting—we must develop instructional practices to promote the meaning-making and differentiated approach. This is especially important as we consider the possibility of more distance learning scenarios in the future (Preston, 2020). Blended learning's mix or "blend" of face-to-face instruction and online experiences enhances learning through flexible pacing and differentiated approaches to address diverse learning modalities and ensure all students have access to rigorous learning opportunities.

The differentiated and highly individualized nature of blended learning lends itself perfectly to the constructivist learning approach by giving students ownership over their learning and allowing them to learn through discovery. Constructivist learning has been championed by education researchers such as Vygotsky, Piaget, and Dewey for decades. It is built on the idea that learners make meaning by building new learning experiences on their previous knowledge and experiences. Researcher Ültanır (2012) argues that "real understanding is only constructed based on learners' previous experience and background knowledge."

> *The differentiated and highly individualized nature of blended learning lends itself perfectly to the constructivist learning approach by giving students ownership over their learning and allowing them to learn through discovery.*

The blended learning model makes it possible to give each student this kind of ownership over their own learning, allowing them to learn through discovery and "construct their own new understandings or knowledge through the interaction of what they already believe and the ideas, events, and activities with which they come into contact" (Ültanır, 2012, p. 195). Throughout the book, we will focus on developing blended learning opportunities that support this meaning-making approach rather than simply using technology as a platform for traditional classroom practices.

> *In the blended learning classroom, students drive the learning process through discovery and by exploring content and how it builds on their previous knowledge.*

BLENDED VS. DISTANCE LEARNING

It is important to distinguish blended learning from distance learning, which offers instruction similar to the classroom experience in an entirely online setting. Courses taken virtually are examples of distance learning, while blended learning mixes "face-to-face classrooms, live e-learning, and self-paced learning" (Singh, 2003). Distance learning may include live instruction online and self-paced learning, but it lacks the face-to-face classroom and physical exploration components such as manipulatives and lab experiments that are critical for many learning modalities. As Singh (2003) explained:

> Learning requirements and preferences of each learner tend to be different. Organizations must use a blend of learning approaches in their strategies to get the right content in the right format to the right people at the right time. Blended learning combines multiple delivery media that are designed to complement each other and promote learning and application-learned behavior. . . . The concept of blended learning is rooted in the idea that learning is not just a one-time event—learning is a continuous process. Blending provides various benefits over using any single learning delivery medium alone. (p. 52)

When implemented with fidelity, blended learning also offers greater balance between teaching and planning. Differentiated, rigorous learning opportunities involve more planning but less direct instruction in the classroom, so the teacher becomes a facilitator of learning and has more time to plan during school hours. This approach enhances learning for students as they learn through collaborative and constructivist learning activities. In addition, it fosters workload sustainability for teachers. Chapter 5 will address sustainability in more detail.

BLENDED LEARNING FOR SOCIAL JUSTICE

As technology has become more prevalent in classrooms over the years, many schools in affluent communities have adopted collaborative and constructivist learning opportunities that facilitate creative thinking and problem solving, while schools in communities with a lower socioeconomic status have focused on basic skills training to help students catch up on skills needed for graduation. While both are important, this discrepancy creates a clearer path toward leadership for students in the affluent schools. To ensure all students are successful, we must incorporate collaborative and constructivist learning opportunities in all classrooms and not wait until all basic skills are mastered. Utilize the power of blended learning to achieve both. Our students cannot afford to wait for those opportunities.

Moreover, it is critical to understand the importance and positive impact of blended learning on students. Aside from it being an effective approach to equity in the classroom, researchers Ling et al. (2010) have found that student satisfaction with the blended learning approach is very high. Blended learning can be a powerful tool to help students understand instructional content and apply it to real-world challenges that are critical for 21st century learning (Beckem & Watkins, 2012). Researchers cite the enhanced learning experience blended learning provides and the positive feedback received from students using the approach. Bonk and Graham (2004) thus highlight the many merits of blended learning for both teachers and students, including "(1) pedagogical richness, (2) access to knowledge, (3) social interaction, (4) personal agency, (5) cost effectiveness, and (6) ease of revision" (p. 7). The merits—particularly the first four—reinforce the potential of blended learning to transform the educational experience for students through constructivist learning opportunities.

Student mastery of course content and the development of critical thinking skills, and not technology, must remain the focus of any instructional plan.

Blended learning is not the result or goal of effective instruction, but rather an approach to help students understand content through a constructivist approach and, at a deeper level, through increased levels of individualized differentiation and a self-starting model. Student mastery of course content and the development of critical thinking skills, and not technology, must remain the focus of any instructional plan.

TECH TIP

To maintain the focus on instruction over technology, avoid initially implementing blended learning as a one-on-one model in which every student has a computer at one time. Without proper training and support, that may lead to an overemphasis on technology. Instead, begin with three students for each computer and rotate through activities to ensure that instruction is front and center. As students and teachers get used to using technology as needed for learning, more devices can be introduced. This also reduces the initial investment in technology needed to begin an effective blended learning program with instructional technology.

FOUR BLENDED LEARNING MODELS

The four blended learning models we will build into our professional development plan are the station rotation model, the flex model, the enriched-virtual model, and the flipped classroom. Not only are these models some of the most researched, but they also integrate high levels of differentiation and data-based student assessment. That means that teachers utilizing these blended learning models will be better equipped to ensure student success.

Rotation Model: This model allows students to rotate through stations (e.g., direct instruction, collaborative, independent learning stations), so they can experience the instructional content through different approaches. This offers multiple opportunities for students to make meaning of the content. In the rotation model, "students rotate on a fixed schedule or at the teacher's discretion between learning modalities, at least one of which is online learning. Other modalities might include activities such as small group or full class instruction, group projects, individual tutoring, and pencil and paper assignments" (Innosight Institute, 2012, p. 8).

Flex Model: In the flex model, "content and instruction are delivered primarily by the Internet, [and] students move on an individually customized, fluid schedule" (Innosight Institute, 2012, p. 12). Each student moves through the learning at their own pace, which offers students more autonomy over how they use their time. Moreover, teachers are able to provide students with more opportunities for instructional support when they need it. When implementing this model, keep in mind that students will be in different stages of the learning process at different times, no longer working on activities or assignments in unison; this can create challenges around classroom transitions and classroom management. Unlike the rotation model, which can be set up with varying numbers of devices at each station, the flex model and the others rely more heavily on a one-to-one device-to-student ratio since access to instruction will be primarily through the device.

The Enriched Virtual Model: The enriched virtual model is essentially what we have come to call "hybrid learning" in 2020. In this model, "students divide their time between attending a brick-and-mortar campus and learning remotely using online delivery of content and instruction" (Innosight Institute, 2012, p. 15).

Flipped-Classroom Model: In the flipped-classroom model, students use instructional videos and readings on their own time to prepare for in-class application. In the classroom, students engage in collaborative activities to apply their learning (Jdaitawi, 2019). Essentially, there is a flip because instruction occurs at home and application occurs in class, instead of the more traditional approach of instruction in the class followed by application at home.

Consider which model most closely resembles the approach educators at your school utilized during distance learning. Review your responses in Figure 1.2 to determine if the model you used in distance learning is the most effective choice for the transition to blended learning. Regardless of the model chosen, multiple delivery methods for content can lead to greater mastery for students with varying learning modalities, while a continuous learning cycle promotes a growth mindset focused on student-driven learning. The high levels of flexibility afforded by the blended learning approach also give students several opportunities for mastery and understanding.

ENHANCING CONCEPTUAL UNDERSTANDING AND CONSTRUCTIVIST LEARNING THROUGH BLENDED LEARNING

It may be difficult for students to access opportunities for higher-order thinking unless blended learning programs are specifically designed to incorporate conceptual understanding and constructivist learning opportunities. Rigorous learning activities create opportunities for students to develop this deeper understanding of the content. A constructivist approach allows students to access this deeper understanding through a variety of methods based on learning modalities and student background.

Students from different socioeconomic, racial, and cultural backgrounds construct meanings based on their own learning modalities during self-learning, and opportunities to inform meaning-making are enhanced through peer collaboration. Blended learning focuses heavily on these ideas and is centered on giving students choice in approach and timing (Cronjé, 2010). Students need to develop a constructivist approach to be successful in a blended learning environment, as Cronjé's research suggests. The opportunity to make meaning at your own pace and through your own learning modalities demonstrates the constructivist learning approaches championed by blended learning. This is particularly evident in the freedom to choose learning styles afforded by the blended learning model.

In blended learning, the teacher's role shifts from being the purveyor of knowledge to being a *facilitator* as students take charge of their own learning. As Ültanır (2012) explains, the teacher's role as facilitator "represents a sharing of the power and responsibility in the room. . . . When the instructor consciously removes herself/himself from the 'centre' of the room, students are empowered to exercise their volition and engage in activities that meet their interests." In other words, students take ownership of their own learning, and teachers allow them to practice autonomy and discovery in the classroom. Through collaborative and constructivist learning opportunities facilitated through a blended learning approach, we can equip students with the skills needed to take charge of their learning, access more rigorous content, and become active lifelong learners.

Not only does this approach build student capacity and foster a classroom environment built on high expectations and care, it has tremendous implications for culturally responsive pedagogy critical for students from all backgrounds to access learning and be successful. In *Culturally Responsive Teaching and the Brain*, Zaretta Hammond (2014) explains,

> The ultimate goal [of culturally responsive teaching] is to help students take over the reins of their learning. This is the social justice aspect of culturally responsive teaching. The first step toward independent learning is acquiring the tools to be more data driven in one's

decision-making about learning tactics and strategies. Dependent learners have been conditioned to be passive when it comes to making decisions about their learning moves. They have relied on the teacher to tell them what to do next. If they are to become more independent, we have to provide them with the tools. (p. 100)

> Through collaborative and constructivist learning opportunities facilitated through a blended learning approach, we can equip students with the skills needed to take charge of their learning, access more rigorous content, and become active lifelong learners.

Yilmaz (2008) shares a similar understanding of the teacher as a facilitator in a constructivist classroom environment:

Constructivist teaching affords learners meaningful, concrete experiences in which they can look for patterns, construct their own questions, and structure their own models, concepts, and strategies. The classroom becomes a micro-society in which learners jointly engage in activity, discourse, and reflection. (p. 169)

With increased access to technology, the teacher is no longer the sole keeper of knowledge in the classroom: every student can access knowledge. However, the teacher's expertise is required to create rigorous learning opportunities that engage students and encourage thought-provoking discussions, establish efficient routines and procedures that maximize learning, and ensure differentiated support for every student.

Let's revisit the distance learning applications of the instructional practices you listed in Figure 1.2 with the added context of conceptual understanding and constructivist learning. This will give us an opportunity to discuss how we can implement these learning approaches effectively in a blended learning classroom. With your faculty and leadership team, reflect on how the instructional practices in Figure 1.4 can utilize instructional technology to enhance conceptual understanding and constructivist learning. Keep this and your conclusions from Figure 1.2 in mind as we get closer to developing an organizational instructional vision based on the return to the classroom from distance learning.

Of the practices listed in Figure 1.4, effective questioning on highly rigorous learning opportunities drives rigorous

FIGURE 1.4 ● Enhancing Conceptual Understanding and Constructivist Learning

INSTRUCTIONAL PRACTICE	HOW TO ENHANCE CONCEPTUAL UNDERSTANDING AND CONSTRUCTIVIST LEARNING	HOW INSTRUCTIONAL TECHNOLOGY CAN SUPPORT THIS EFFORT
Differentiated supports for equitable access		
Actionable feedback to students		
Effective questioning to facilitate constructivist learning		
Student collaboration		
Assessments to gather actionable data		
Highly rigorous learning opportunities		

 Figure 1.4 is available as a downloadable template on the Companion Website at Resources.Corwin.com/BlendedLearningPlanner.

learning and support. With access to instructional technology, students have the resources to research and analyze complex ideas and draw conclusions; it is critical for teachers to develop rigorous, higher-ordering thinking prompts that take advantage of students' access to these resources. Figure 1.5 shows how rigorous learning opportunities supported by effective questioning create access to rich learning experiences. Only both elements implemented together can set the groundwork for meaningful impacts from the other practices.

For some guidance on developing high-level questioning, consider using Dr. Norman Webb's Depth of Knowledge framework to design rigorous learning prompts.

FIGURE 1.5 ● Impact of Rigorous Prompts and High-level Questioning

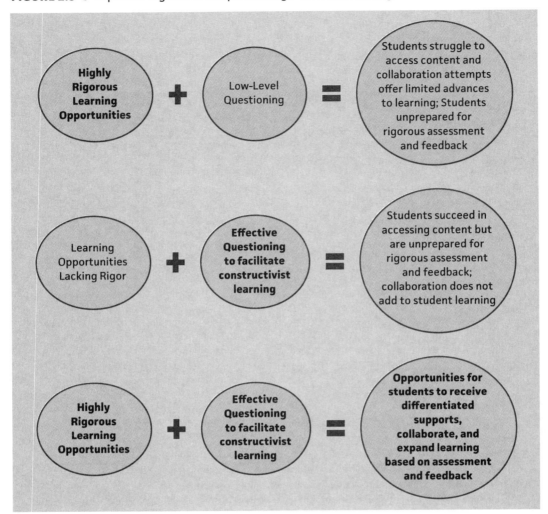

LEVERAGING BLENDED LEARNING TO CLOSE THE ACHIEVEMENT GAP

A focus on blended learning is important from a social justice perspective because of the potential educational technology has for addressing learning gaps for students from low socioeconomic backgrounds. Differentiated instruction that includes individualized supports can help all students in blended learning classrooms succeed regardless of background.

If individualized instruction and constructivist learning go underutilized in urban schools, the achievement gap between students from affluent communities and students from neighborhoods with a low socioeconomic status will further widen.

The impact of blended learning on social justice also applies to disadvantaged students in under-resourced schools. Prominent schools in affluent areas have begun to utilize the blended learning approach, giving their students opportunities to engage with technology and to become self-starters who take ownership of their learning; urban schools must give students from all socioeconomic backgrounds the same opportunities (Herold, 2014). The constructivist learning opportunities and flexibility in learning options offered in affluent schools contrast sharply with the structured timelines and extensive direct instruction that characterize some schools in less affluent socioeconomic areas. This latter approach also reinforces the notion of students as dependent learners, a concept Hammond (2014) strongly advises against as part of culturally responsive pedagogy. A lack of available resources and a desire to help students quickly get caught up with basic skills needed for graduation often drive this approach, with constructivist learning opportunities deemed too time-consuming in the classroom. Guiding students through the meaning-making process does certainly take more time than sharing content in a direct instruction format, but it maximizes internalization of learning for application, deeper understanding, and retention. This stark difference in approach can dramatically widen the achievement gap as students in affluent areas are given more opportunities to become critical thinkers and leaders.

Your district does not need to have a device for every student to implement blended learning well. Like we saw in the tech tip early on in Chapter 1, starting with about one device for every three students will keep the focus on instruction and reduce your initial investment in technology.

TECH TIP

As mentioned in the previous tech tip, begin with fewer devices than the number of students. Not every station needs to have computers. Reinforce the notion that computers are a resource to support learning just like textbooks and other instructional materials. Traditional learning materials can still have a place in these models.

If individualized instruction and constructivist learning go underutilized in urban schools, the achievement gap between students from affluent communities and students from neighborhoods with a low socioeconomic status will widen further. With your leadership team, discuss how instructional technology can impact the achievement gap using Figure 1.6. These responses will guide teams with designing learning plans that meet the needs of *all* students.

FIGURE 1.6 ● Impacting the Achievement Gap

HOW INSTRUCTIONAL TECHNOLOGY CAN CLOSE THE ACHIEVEMENT GAP	HOW INSTRUCTIONAL TECHNOLOGY CAN WIDEN THE ACHIEVEMENT GAP

 Figure 1.6 is available as a downloadable template on the Companion Website at Resources.Corwin.com/BlendedLearningPlanner.

As its use grows, blended learning has the potential to address several challenges in classrooms, including class size, student time on task, and limited individualized learning experiences. This can have a dramatic impact on equity in education as more students from across the world gain access to a wide variety of educational resources and opportunities. Students from various schools can collaborate, engage in dialogue, and access similar tools. They can connect remotely to resources not immediately available in their neighborhoods and be exposed to different experiences and perspectives to further extend constructivist learning opportunities.

DISTANCE VS. BLENDED LEARNING

Distance learning addresses some of the learning needs of students, but the blended learning approach further enhances learning by meeting the needs of students with different learning modalities, including those who require hands-on experience. Manipulatives and other materials are combined with digital resources in a blended learning classroom to maximize learning. In the same way that some adult learners better access information on paper documents than digital ones, some students are more successful when digital resources are combined with other classroom materials.

As technology usage and the self-starting approach ramp up across schools and companies, all students need opportunities to create and explore with technology, so they are prepared for the workforce (Cronjé, 2010). However, simply providing students access to technology is not enough; teachers must be well-prepared to utilize technology to enhance learning experiences and offer effective instruction, especially to students who are "digital natives" and experienced technology users.

BLENDED LEARNING FOR SOCIAL JUSTICE

How you will ensure that all students have access to instructional technology at home? You may consider loaning out Chromebooks or laptops (Chromebooks tend to be less expensive and easier to manage) and can even insure them for minimal cost in case of damage.

BRINGING IT ALL TOGETHER

Bringing together the most effective elements of distance learning and the traditional classroom in your school and district and framing them in the context of constructivist learning and conceptual understanding creates a powerful formula for establishing a highly effective blended learning program designed to meet the needs of each individual student. As we delve deeper into the contributions of distance learning to the blended learning classroom, we will better understand how instructional technology, when coupled with exceptional instruction, can help all students access rigorous content and prepare for the careers of the future.

FIGURE 1.7 ● Bringing Together the Elements of an Effective Blended Learning Classroom

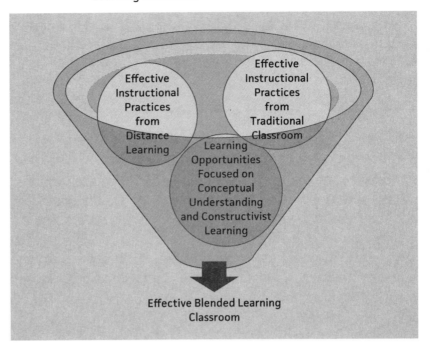

Effective Instructional Practices from Distance Learning

Effective Instructional Practices from Traditional Classroom

Learning Opportunities Focused on Conceptual Understanding and Constructivist Learning

Effective Blended Learning Classroom

Review your findings from the interactive figures in this chapter; integrating these elements requires careful planning and a strong educator support network to share best practices and resources as part of a comprehensive professional development plan, which we will explore in depth in Chapters 3–5. Schools that spend time and effort to establish and maintain these networks early on will consistently increase the effectiveness of their instructional programs. For many districts, the sudden shift to distance learning spurred by the COVID-19 pandemic left little time for professional development on constructivist learning; instead, training focused largely on mastering the instructional technology programs required for distance learning. The transition from distance learning to blended learning in the classroom, however, will require thoughtful professional development programs focused on constructivist learning.

Key Takeaways

In this chapter, we explored how

- Instructional practices from the distance learning experience can supplement effective teaching in a traditional classroom environment to inform a successful blended learning program.

- Blended learning can enhance conceptual understanding and constructivist learning to increase rigor and offer differentiated supports to ensure all students succeed.

- A collaborative approach to reflection and planning will facilitate the successful implementation of your organization's blended learning program.

The next chapter will build on these ideas by discussing the critical elements of adult learning needed to effectively begin the transition from distance to blended learning.

Rethinking Professional Development in Blended Learning

This chapter uses the framework for a blended learning program from the previous chapter to inform the establishment of a robust professional development (PD) program that addresses the shift from distance to blended learning. The program will specifically address the use of professional learning communities (PLCs), technology integration, research on blended learning theory, effective blended learning models, and sustainability.

A WORD ON PROFESSIONAL DEVELOPMENT LEADERSHIP

A PD program is only as effective as how well it is received by participants. One of the best ways to increase buy-in, engagement, and credibility is to co-plan and co-lead PD with teachers and other classroom practitioners. Doing so builds their leadership capacity, while reinforcing the notion that training is closely tied and applicable to classrooms. For these reasons, all PD planning recommendations and implementation strategies mentioned in this book should be applied with a leadership team comprised of stakeholders in the classroom and in school and district leadership roles. Consider how you create this PD leadership team as you continue diving into this chapter.

One of the best ways to increase PD program buy-in, and therefore its effectiveness, is to co-plan and co-lead the PD with teachers.

Part I: A New Vision for Learning and Professional Development

---

Chapter 1: **Elements of an Effective Blended Learning Classroom**

- Effective instructional practices from distance learning
- Effective instructional practices from the traditional classroom
- A focus on conceptual understanding and constructivist learning

Which come from...

Chapter 2: **Planning an Effective PD Program**

- Peer observations in BL classrooms *(tips in Chapters 3 & 5)*
- PLCs focused on best practices *(tips in Chapters 3 & 4)*
- Tech integration with a focus on instruction *(tips in Chapters 3 & 4)*
- Research on BL theory and effective practices *(tips in Chapters 4 & 5)*
- Analysis of effective models in a BL classroom *(tips in Chapter 5)*
- Teacher workload sustainability *(tips in Chapter 5)*

That focuses on...

Part II: Applying PD Strategies to Instructional Practice

CH. 3: **RIGOROUS LEARNING FOR ALL**	*CH. 4:* **PERSONALIZED ASSESSMENT & FEEDBACK**	*CH. 5:* **CLASSROOM CULTURE**
• Differentiation for equitable access • Constructivist learning opportunities • Effective questioning • Student collaboration	• Assessments to gather actionable data • Actionable feedback for all students • Facilitating self-monitoring • Peer feedback	• Digital citizenship training • Learning environments in a BL model • A collaborative learning culture • Tech integration and management

And leads to...

Part III: Bringing Training and Application Together in One Cohesive Program

---

Conclusion: *Bringing It All Together*

- Creating a vision based on key takeaways
- Focused leadership during the transition
- Building your professional development team
- Collaborating with students and parents as stakeholders
- Soliciting feedback on distance learning
- Sharing blended learning impact on student learning
- Preparing students for a new world

SHIFTING PROFESSIONAL DEVELOPMENT METHODOLOGY

A successful transition from distance to blended learning in the classroom requires a comprehensive PD program designed to combine the most effective elements of in-person and online instruction. Districts will need to carefully evaluate their philosophy for learning to determine their vision of PD. Most importantly, your PD vision and plan must maintain a sustained focus on instruction, not resources. Rather than training teachers on operating instructional technology, blended learning PD must focus on utilizing instructional technology to develop rigorous, constructivist learning experiences that pique students' intellectual curiosity and prepare them to be lifelong learners. Beginning this transition requires careful analysis of what PD currently looks like and how it supports the district's or school's vision for learning. Use Figure 2.1 to start this discussion with your faculty and leadership teams.

If a widespread transition to blended learning is your ultimate goal, your organization's vision for PD must prioritize collaborative learning and constructivist thinking through the incorporation of instructional technology.

. . . .

Most importantly, your PD vision and plan must maintain
a sustained focus on instruction, not resources.

. . . .

FIGURE 2.1 ● Your Vision for Professional Development

What is your school's or district's current vision for professional development?	
In what ways does the current professional development vision foster collaborative learning and constructivist thinking?	
How, if at all, has the school's (or district's) vision been impacted by the distance learning experience?	
What updates should be explored as a result to ensure rigorous, differentiated learning and equity for all students?	

 Figure 2.1 is available as a downloadable template on the Companion Website at Resources.Corwin.com/BlendedLearningPlanner.

Part II will explore the process for establishing a PD program to address these critical elements. The pedagogical philosophies behind collaborative learning and constructivist thinking facilitate rigorous, differentiated experiences for students, setting the framework for instructional technology to maximize learning impact. If this vision for learning is not clearly established as the driving force behind all PD, it becomes exceedingly easy for other priorities to dominate organization-wide training. The most likely culprits will be the instructional technology resources themselves as many educators will need support using them. However, research shows that effective instruction—not instructional technology resources—must be the focus of a successful instructional program (Herring, 2004). While we need to support teachers in learning how to utilize instructional technology, our focus must remain on the type of learning that the technology will enable. The rapid transition to distance learning incentivized many districts to focus on instructional resource training, but the shift to blended learning is an opportunity to revisit and reset the vision for learning.

BLENDED LEARNING FOR SOCIAL JUSTICE

As you discuss your vision for learning, be sure to prioritize social justice and that all students are successful as part of your vision. A vision statement that makes assumptions about students' access to technology or prior knowledge may leave some students behind, which runs counter to the purpose of differentiated learning.

Teachers require extensive training to prepare students for collaboration in class and online, especially because many students will be experiencing online collaboration for the first time. In addition to technical training, teachers must understand the characteristics of learning activities taught through an online approach rather when taught exclusively in-person. They must also teach digital citizenship, preferably using a blended approach. Since these critical understandings are not subject specific and apply to all blended classrooms, it is essential for these student trainings to be discussed and agreed upon *by the entire school* and incorporated into the schoolwide expectations for students.

TECH TIP

There is a fine balance between monitoring technology use to safeguard students and establishing a perceived culture of mistrust. Establish protocols to keep students safe and use the strategies in Chapter 5 to reinforce expectations rather than investing in expensive in-class monitoring programs.

Implementing blended learning with fidelity is challenging. The multitasked classroom environment can be difficult to plan for and manage, technical difficulties can derail wonderful lessons, and achieving conceptual understanding through collaboration can be a challenge to design. Since blended learning approach is relatively new in most districts, PD to utilize it is still being developed and is in high demand. As Owston and York (2012) explain, "the main caveat in expanding blended learning . . . is that instructors must be more adequately prepared to teach in this format." Teacher training for traditional classroom instruction does not necessarily transfer seamlessly to the blended learning model, dispelling the notion that an effective traditional classroom teacher is immediately ready to lead a blended learning classroom (Davis & Rose, 2007, p. 7). This finding emphasizes the importance of training specific for blended learning to ensure effective implementation.

TECH TIP

Prioritize instructional strategies, not technology, during blended learning PD. However, have technical answers ready to facilitate learning during PD. For example, if you are using polling software to gather input from teachers to inform differentiation, include a *how-to video* via a screencast link in the PD materials so teachers can understand how to use polling in their classrooms to gather formative data. Teachers can review them later, in addition to attending an optional tech support session later. The how-to video will create more access to the tool, while maintaining the focus of the session on the instructional practice.

In addition, the quality of blended learning coursework must be measured and considered when establishing a blended learning program. To assist in the development of measures to assess program quality, the Aurora Institute (formerly the International Association for K–12 Online Learning, or iNACOL) developed standards that provide guidance for high-quality blended learning instruction. These standards, which describe elements of effective blended learning instruction, can be found in the *National Standards for Quality Online Teaching* (2011). They are designed to measure effectiveness in academic content, resource utilization, data analysis, instructional strategies, and assessment. Although the inclusion of standards is helpful in identifying what effective blended learning implementation looks like, it does not provide explicit guidance on the training educators need to address the standards.

BLENDED LEARNING FOR SOCIAL JUSTICE

Some parents will be unfamiliar with blended learning philosophy and instructional technology and may be apprehensive about computers in the classroom. Create opportunities for parents to learn more about blended learning so they can support student learning at home. Some parents may have work schedules that prevent them from attending meetings or observations during the day, so after-school opportunities should also be offered. Be sure to invite translators to the trainings to ensure equitable access for all participants.

GATHERING THE DATA

As you build out your PD topics, make sure that they are centered around instructional practice and based on data and teacher needs in your school. Gather data from teacher observations, blended learning programs, and feedback from teachers' distance learning experience. Doing so will ensure that PD supports the greatest areas of growth and blended learning programs support students' highest needs. Establishing and implementing a plan that addresses all these considerations requires planning, reflection, and an unflinching focus on student achievement. It must also be highly aligned to the organization's philosophy for blended learning PD focused on collaborative learning and constructivist thinking using instructional technology upon reopening schools. We will explore an overview of the planning process in this chapter before the deeper analysis in Part II.

Data-driven planning can generate buy-in for the PD plan as well as maximize the impact of learning by targeting areas of need. Using a wide variety of data sources adds validity to the plan, while taking multiple perspectives into consideration. Some data sources to consider include

- Qualitative and quantitative data from teacher observations using a protocol

- Student performance metrics derived from blended learning instructional apps

- Teacher feedback on effective practices from distance learning, which can be gathered in meetings and from surveys
- Feedback from students and families on strategies that supported learning

DEVELOPING A PROFESSIONAL DEVELOPMENT PLAN WITH A SUSTAINED FOCUS ON INSTRUCTION

Begin the process of developing a comprehensive blended learning PD program by reviewing your team's PD vision in Figure 2.1. Identify elements of distance learning that were successful in advancing student learning. Assess where these findings fit in your organization's vision for student learning. Do collaborative learning and constructivist thinking fit in the learning philosophy for your organization? Does the philosophy need to be revisited to better frame a blended learning PD program? Your review can also identify data points to inform PD topics and best practices. Most importantly, the plan must maintain a sustained focus on instruction, not resources.

DISTANCE VS. BLENDED LEARNING

For many districts, the rapid and sudden transition to distance learning led to a rollout of resources for teachers to use online with trainings and webinars on how to use the resources. Most districts did not have time to implement PD on instructional techniques. PD on effective instruction will be absolutely essential for successful blended learning implementation. Be sure this step is prioritized.

Focus on critical instructional practices such as effective questioning and actionable feedback in PD and then introduce instructional technology to support the successful implementation of those practices. Teachers as learners will experience the instructional technology firsthand and will have the context required for successful implementation in their own classrooms. Educators who need additional technical support to use the resources can benefit from training videos or from in-person, supplemental, and optional follow-up sessions for technical support. Use your findings in Figure 2.1 to write down your organization's PD vision at the top of Figure 2.2. With your task force, review your findings from Figures 1.2, 1.4, and 1.6, along with the data you've collected in your school or district, to inform the topics and details for implementation in Figure 2.2.

FIGURE 2.2 ● Your Professional Development Plan

YOUR PROFESSIONAL DEVELOPMENT VISION FOR STUDENT LEARNING;				
PROFESSIONAL DEVELOPMENT TOPIC	**DATA INFORMING INCLUSION OF THIS TOPIC**	**HOW IT WILL FOSTER COLLABORATIVE LEARNING**	**HOW IT WILL FOSTER CONSTRUCTIVIST THINKING**	**INSTRUCTIONAL TECHNOLOGY FROM DISTANCE LEARNING TO INCORPORATE**
Sample: Effective questioning practices	Classroom observations documenting question distribution and rigor level	Rigorous questions that prompt exploration and detailed explanation facilitate opportunities for students to collaborate on research and analysis	Rigorous questions explored through collaboration foster discovery and meaning-making	Collaborative online documents such as the Google Suite for Education

 Figure 2.2 is available as a downloadable template on the Companion Website at Resources.Corwin .com/BlendedLearningPlanner.

Be sure to include stakeholders in the planning process and include their experiences as an integral part of the transition from distance learning. Remember that the transition to distance learning was done out of necessity and did not require buy-in from stakeholders; the transition to blended learning, however, will require buy-in from stakeholders and focused leadership. Without buy-in, expect a return to the traditional instructional model used before distance learning. Use Figure 2.3 to plan how you will generate buy-in from stakeholders to ensure successful implementation.

FIGURE 2.3 ● Generating Buy-In

How will you leverage teachers' distance learning experience to generate buy-in for blended learning implementation?	
What data points will you gather to support blended learning implementation?	
Describe the critical mass needed to facilitate blended learning implementation.	
What potential challenges might you encounter? How will you address them?	

 Figure 2.3 is available as a downloadable template on the Companion Website at Resources.Corwin.com/BlendedLearningPlanner.

∙ ∙

Remember that the transition to distance learning was done out of necessity and did not require buy-in from stakeholders; the transition to blended learning, however, will require buy-in from stakeholders and focused leadership.

∙ ∙

TEACHER-LED PD THAT OFFERS LEADERSHIP OPPORTUNITIES AND INCREASED BUY-IN

Opportunities for professional growth and leadership are part of the culture of any successful organization. This applies to schools and districts as well; educators crave leadership opportunities, especially when they have expertise others can benefit from. Invite teachers to share successes from their distance learning experience that they believe can apply to a blended learning setting. As an organizational leader, it is essential to review the findings in Figure 2.2 in the previous section and develop a plan to

- Differentiate professional learning based on pedagogical needs
- Create opportunities for teachers to demonstrate leadership in PD

To differentiate professional learning, you will first need to evaluate data on strengths and areas of growth. These can come from classroom observations, teacher and student feedback, distance learning experiences, and PD session evaluations. Collaboratively, identify data points that can be used to inform PD and select the pedagogical practices teachers will need additional support with and use these as the framework for PD planning. Be sure to focus on pedagogical over technical expertise when differentiating to emphasize the priority of instructional practice over instructional technology. Instructional technology is integrated into effective teaching to enhance student learning, but it must always play a supporting role to effective teaching.

Collaborating with teachers to share their expertise when planning PD will also pay dividends in training effectiveness. Connect with teachers who demonstrate proficiency in instructional practices and work with them to design and lead PD. In your planning conversations, discuss how the effective instructional practice transferred to distance learning and how, if at all, it can apply to blended learning. Teachers will appreciate the opportunity to share their expertise, develop leadership skills, and reinforce the collaborative nature of learning on campus.

Teachers also need formal opportunities to evaluate models, develop skills, and work through anticipated challenges using

- Peer observations in blended learning classrooms
- PLCs focused on best practices

- Technology integration, including a focus on instruction
- Research on blended learning theory and effective practices
- Detailed analysis of effective models in a blended learning classroom
- Understanding how to develop strategies and resources to ensure sustainability of the lesson planning workload and continuous direct instruction in some station models

We will explore how these opportunities can enhance an effective blended learning PD program that brings the organizational vision to life and build on strengths of educators.

PEER OBSERVATIONS IN
BLENDED LEARNING CLASSROOMS

Observing effective models in action is a critical part of a comprehensive PD plan. For many districts, this element will be missing from their rapidly implemented distance learning experience, making its inclusion in blended learning all the more important. It is essential to create opportunities to observe classrooms to see different models in practice and to analyze the benefits and drawbacks of each.

Many school administrators are in the challenging position of serving as instructional leaders without having directly experienced the type of instruction they are supporting, which means they must continually learn about effective blended learning to support teachers. More classroom instructors experienced with blended learning will become administrators in time, but the gap between teacher and administrator experience levels is currently wide. Observations and feedback from instructors can inform the focus of the analysis to ensure the greatest possible impact on instruction. Observation data can be combined with feedback from students and parents, a critical element often missed in identifying focus areas, to be used to inform planning schoolwide PD. By building a collaborative learning network, schools can rapidly improve blended learning instruction and contribute to the body of research for other schools to benefit from.

Many school administrators are in the challenging position of serving as instructional leaders without having directly experienced the type of instruction they are supporting, which means they must continually learn about effective blended learning to support teachers.

BLENDED LEARNING FOR SOCIAL JUSTICE

As teams observe instructional technology use in classrooms, look for trends in usage and support. Are all students getting equitable access to instructional technology, including those less experienced with using devices? What supports are in place to ensure equitable access?

To maximize the impact of peer observations, the team can develop a list of instructional practices to look for or potential approaches to challenges faced in other classrooms. Ideally, the teachers opening their classrooms for observation will make time for questions or advice after the observations. This critical step will help observers make the most of this opportunity. Use Figure 2.4 to help teachers plan for their peer observations and align focus areas to the PD topics highlighted in Figure 2.2 to reinforce takeaways and to build a common theme throughout different forms of professional learning. These planning notes will be extremely beneficial when we apply PD to instructional practice in more detail in the next chapter.

Schools need to plan both learning goals and logistics around peer observations to ensure they are impactful. Specific learning goals that align to school goals must be discussed, keeping in mind that blended learning serves as an approach to delivering content and not the content itself. Establishing context before observations can emphasize this approach and lead to more impactful learning. Teachers should have autonomy in determining how the learnings will impact their classroom instruction, while staying true to the schoolwide goals.

FIGURE 2.4 ● Peer Observation Planning Template for Teachers

Schoolwide learning goals	
Specific instructional strategies to look for in a blended learning classroom	
Best practice to address a challenge in my classroom	
Evidence of its effectiveness for student learning	
Questions for post-observation	
Observed resource I want to learn more about	

 Figure 2.4 is available as a downloadable template on the Companion Website at Resources.Corwin.com/BlendedLearningPlanner.

TECH TIP

Consider using a digital observation tool to quickly consolidate observation data. You can use an online form such as Google Forms or Survey Monkey to capture both qualitative and quantitative data. The quantitative data points can be used to sort and filter notes, and once this step is done, you can review qualitative notes in more detail. For example, you can export the results to a spreadsheet, filter to see all science class observations, and look for patterns and trends in those observations. This can inform next steps for differentiated support.

The school schedule might be reworked to create opportunities for observation, and a system must be in place for identifying which classrooms to observe and for what purpose. Logistics such as classroom coverage must be arranged and videotaping options discussed to support logistics. A system to organize and store observed best practices with justifications can be helpful. Increased comfort with videoconferencing from the distance learning experience may also create opportunities for virtual observations, which can address logistical challenges, as well as minimize disruptions for the observed classroom. In their research on remote observations, Mac Mahon et al. (2019) explain, "Without the physical presence of an observer, the consequent reduction in reactivity enabled a more authentic classroom context, resulting in more 'natural' behaviour from pupils, along with reduced apprehension and nervousness among student teachers." To do this, schools will first need to establish systems to facilitate regular remote observation, such as camera and microphone placements to capture both teacher and student voice and action.

DISTANCE VS. BLENDED LEARNING

What did classroom observations look like during distance learning? We are used to conducting observations in person in the classroom, and with distance learning, observations became limited to other educators joining the virtual classroom through videoconferencing. Student engagement was more challenging to assess, especially in multiple breakout rooms. With blended learning, observations can once again be done in the physical classroom, though observation of students' online work as well will give better insight on their success.

PROFESSIONAL LEARNING COMMUNITIES

PLCs are very popular in some schools and districts. Whether you choose PLCs or another collaborative model in your organization, a process for educators to systemically share best practices, discuss common challenges, and build collective capacity is an essential part of an effective blended learning PD program. Blended learning implementation is in its infancy compared to traditional classroom instruction, making collaboration between educators critical to identifying best practices, sharing resources, and working through common challenges. This is particularly important for teachers who have limited experience with instructional technology and practices for differentiation and constructivist thinking. The well-structured PLC with a clear vision can have a long-term positive impact on student learning as teaching practices become increasingly refined through regular reflection and analysis. With your task force, reflect on the appropriate steps and considerations for establishing a collaborative learning system in your organization using Figure 2.5.

Blended learning implementation is in its infancy compared to traditional classroom instruction, making collaboration between educators critical to identifying best practices, sharing resources, and working through common challenges.

FIGURE 2.5 ● Professional Learning Community Planning

How are professional learning communities currently perceived in my organization?	
How can I generate buy-in from teachers to actively get involved in collaborative learning?	
How will I create the time and space needed for professional collaboration in my organization?	
How will I ensure that teachers with varying expertise all benefit from the collaboration?	

 Figure 2.5 is available as a downloadable template on the Companion Website at Resources.Corwin.com/BlendedLearningPlanner.

As before, be sure to align the PLC's areas of focus to the PD topics you listed in Figure 2.2, so different learning opportunities inform each other and heighten experiences. Disjointed PLC topics and PD sessions can dilute the focus of the organization's vision for learning, a particularly harmful circumstance when trying to build buy-in for a new instructional framework. Applying PD to PLC implementation will also be addressed in the next chapter.

TECHNOLOGY INTEGRATION

In addition to developing proficiency with various educational apps, teachers and administrators must master data analysis to facilitate differentiation and blended lesson planning to create constructivist and rigorous learning opportunities.

All PD must be driven by effective instructional practices but be able to incorporate technology tools and programs when applicable. Sessions that focus solely on technological resource sharing have not proven to be the most effective form of PD; teachers need context to know how the technology can apply to instruction and student learning. Student learning—the ultimate outcome of teacher growth—must drive PD, with technology supporting that focus. The two should always be presented together.

A PD facilitator can introduce an instructional best practice and give participants an opportunity to experience it in action as a learner. For example, if participants are learning about differentiated small group instruction, the facilitator can offer a prompt that allows participants to identify their expertise level and self-select their small group for differentiated PD. This allows participants to experience the strategy from the perspective of the students and facilitates thinking about effective strategies and considerations. Incorporating an instructional technology resource during this process to enhance learning can show teachers the impact of the tool on student learning. A link with technical directions and screencasts can be made available to teachers, so they can review the logistical requirements necessary to implement the app in their classrooms. Teachers who are comfortable with technology will quickly develop proficiency with the app and begin using it in their classrooms. Those who need additional support can attend an optional workshop available within a couple of days of the PD date, so they can learn how to use the resource shared. Note that the technical directions for using the app are not shared in the PD session, maintaining the commitment to effective instructional practice as the focus of adult learning.

· ·

Student learning—the ultimate outcome of teacher growth—
must drive PD, with technology supporting that focus.
The two should always be presented together.

· ·

Observing instructional technology discussed in action can be a great way to utilize peer observations, once again connecting different types of learning into one common thread. To maximize the impact of PD, consider establishing a system for regular peer observation after trainings to rapidly advance teacher understanding and implementation of effective practice and technology. Use Figure 2.6 to thread different learning opportunities.

Notice that the last column in Figure 2.6 is for additional research because further exploration of a relatively new topic can engage educators and introduce methodologies from

FIGURE 2.6 ● Expanding the Impact of Professional Development Sessions

PROFESSIONAL DEVELOPMENT TOPIC	WHEN TO OFFER OPTIONAL INSTRUCTIONAL TECHNOLOGY REVIEW	PEER OBSERVATION CLASSROOMS TO SHOW STRATEGY IN ACTION	PROFESSIONAL LEARNING COMMUNITY CONNECTION	ADDITIONAL RESEARCH FOR THIS TOPIC

 Figure 2.6 is available as a downloadable template on the Companion Website at Resources.Corwin .com/BlendedLearningPlanner.

sources outside the organization. Like peer observations and PLCs, technology integration application will be a central topic of the next chapter.

TEACHER RESEARCH ON BLENDED LEARNING

Encouraging research as part of the PD program fosters intellectual curiosity, provides support or counterexamples for current practices, and further hones the program to more effectively prepare teachers for effective blended learning instruction. Research can include a variety of sources such as academic papers and classroom observations, but the purpose must always focus on improving the organization's approach to effective instruction through comprehensive PD. Research can come from teachers, school administrators, and district leads; all of these roles bring different perspectives, and their diverse approaches can refine organizational training to generate buy-in and maximize effective instruction. Incorporating research can also facilitate a closer look into how instructional practices need to be adjusted to be effective in a blended learning classroom. If your school or district does not have a culture of research and inquiry, now is the time to start the conversation with stakeholders. Identify educational leaders and create opportunities for them to share findings. Doing so will further validate PD topics, which in turn will accelerate learning throughout the organization.

DETAILED ANALYSIS OF EFFECTIVE MODELS

To support blended learning instructors' professional growth, schools need to identify models and analyze what makes them effective. School leaders can lead this work as part of their own growth as instructional leaders, but the process should build investment through teacher collaboration. The evaluation process can be a great way to unify the school as everyone works together toward a common goal. The review process can also spark an important conversation about a common understanding of effective instructional practice. Districts can begin by identifying schools that utilize blended learning (or classrooms within schools if no schoolwide programs are available). Some can be found on databases focused on blended learning, such as the ones developed by the Christensen Institute. They can also identify research on effective blended learning practices from think tanks focusing on this topic, such as the Aurora Institute.

Throughout the process, it is important to remember that blended learning is a relatively new instructional approach, and no particular model has been proven to be most effective. Several models can be effective if they are implemented with fidelity and after careful planning. Some models, however, are easier to implement for a new blended learning teacher because of their relative resemblance to traditional class-rooms. For example, the station rotation model more closely resembles traditional small-group instruction compared to the flipped classroom model, which relies on students watch-ing recorded lessons by the teacher the night before class in anticipation of practice problems being completed in class the next day. Some teachers use stations in their classrooms even without instructional technology so the transition to a blended station rotation model is not a giant leap. The flipped classroom, however, requires a comprehensive shift in lesson planning, technology implementation, and student training.

BLENDED LEARNING FOR SOCIAL JUSTICE

If you choose to use the flipped classroom model, you must ensure that all students, not most, have access to a device and Internet at home. Chapter 5 describes in detail how schools can support student learning at home using existing devices and grants.

The implementation model must not be chosen without teachers' input and analysis. Understanding the benefits of drawbacks through a constructivist approach is critical for internalization, understanding, and investment. Take the time to analyze and experiment with models together to find the one(s) that fit of your students best. In the process, you will be building teacher capacity for blended learning methodology and leadership.

SUSTAINABILITY

Sustaining a blended learning program is a serious concern for educators, specifically around the demands of differentiated lesson planning and managing both instructional and technical logistics. The blended learning teacher takes a facilitator role during class, which heightens planning demands, but greatly reduces direct instructional time. There are several steps educators can take to make blended learning lesson planning and implementation sustainable and effective.

The blended learning teacher takes a facilitator role during class, which heightens planning demands, but greatly reduces direct instructional time.

First, collaborating on lesson planning can lessen the burden of having to plan multiple lessons for each class in addition to creating opportunities for more interdisciplinary learning experiences for students. When students need particular math skills for a science lesson, for example, teachers can work together to share the planning workload. The resulting lesson will be easier to plan as well as more rigorous because of the interdisciplinary nature of the lesson. Grade level teams can also plan collaboratively. One example that has stayed with me for years is the collaborative planning of two fifth-grade teachers with vastly different teaching styles. Walking from one classroom to the other revealed indisputable evidence of collaborative planning, yet their teaching styles were vastly different. Their lessons were aligned with standards, learning prompts, and student mastery evidence despite differing classroom structures, expectations, and culture. It was a powerful reminder that collaborative planning does not diminish autonomy but has several advantages, including aiding sustainability.

Second, PD must emphasize that differentiating to meet student needs does not require multiple learning activities for each lesson. While some teachers expressed concern about the time it takes to make multiple versions of each lesson, truly effective differentiated learning does not require unique prompts, tasks, and supports for every single learning activity. When designing the learning activities to help students achieve lesson objectives, plan in advance by creating learning prompts with built-in differentiation. Learning opportunities can include prompts for further exploration of the topic, and supports can be incorporated throughout, ensuring students who can benefit from them have access. Separate prompts and activities do not need to be created for each learning opportunity; adjustments to the main prompt can provide the necessary differentiation. Supports can also be linked to one location and new ones can be added as the lessons progress, limiting the need for unique supports for each lesson. This takes time to master, but as planning becomes more robust, the lessons become more impactful, and developing them becomes more efficient.

Utilizing every minute to advance student learning must be an integral part of the school culture and can be a driving force to ensure teachers are consistently ready with learning opportunities for students who do not have the luxury of a lost instructional period.

Another concern around sustainability stems from having to manage instruction and technical challenges, which can quickly exhaust a teacher who frequently needs to redirect students back to learning after technical issues pause the lesson. Several supports can be developed during the planning phase to minimize disruptions to learning by technical challenges. A portion of the teacher's website can be devoted to a support page with short screencasts on how to access materials, troubleshoot login issues, create accounts, review data, and establish online collaboration groups. Students can visit the page to get help when the teacher is not available to assist. The second tier of support can be assigned to student experts in the room who can assist when the self-help page does not resolve the issue.

 TECH TIP

The fifth chapter will explore these supports further, including how to manage technical resources and how to train your tech team to become effective tech leaders in classrooms.

Teachers must be prepared with back-up plans in case school-wide technical issues such as Internet connection loss occur. The back-up plan does not necessarily need to be photocopied versions of the lesson materials: Online materials can be downloaded in advance for offline use, in-person discussion opportunities can be rearranged within a unit, and sessions for goal-setting and planning can be initiated. Utilizing every minute to advance student learning must be an integral part of the school culture and can be a driving force to ensure teachers are consistently ready with learning opportunities for students who do not have the luxury of a lost instructional period.

DISTANCE VS. BLENDED LEARNING

Technical issues can critically hamper instruction in a blended learning classroom just as they can impact distance learning. In a blended learning classroom, however, other resources are at your immediate disposal. Plan for potential technical issues so learning can continue uninterrupted. At least one day of technical difficulties in the school year is a reasonable assumption.

Your PD program can include optional technical sessions to help teachers establish these supports in their classrooms. These sessions can also serve as opportunities for teachers to share and compile their screencasts and other technical supports as there is no need for several teachers to record how-to videos for the same program.

CONSIDERATIONS BEYOND PROFESSIONAL DEVELOPMENT

As you develop your organization's PD plan, consider the following at each step:

- How will this plan differentiate for student learning?
- How will we assess the plan's successful implementation?

- How will we distinguish the plan's implementation in a distance learning setting from implementation in a blended learning setting?

- How will this plan offer leadership opportunities to teachers?

These questions will help us connect PD to other elements of a successful instructional program in the coming chapters. With a thoughtful, differentiated PD program in place that includes multiple approaches to learning such as observation, collaboration, and technical training, your organization will have the framework in place to further explore effective practices in the blended learning classroom.

Key Takeaways

In this chapter, we reviewed how

- The shift from distance to blended learning requires a unique vision for PD

- PD must maintain a sustained focus on instruction, not resources

- Growth opportunities for educators must be prevalent to foster professional learning

Part II will establish best practices for assessing the effectiveness of learning driven by the PD program to ensure actionable data inform next steps for differentiated support.

Applying Professional Development Strategies to Instructional Practice

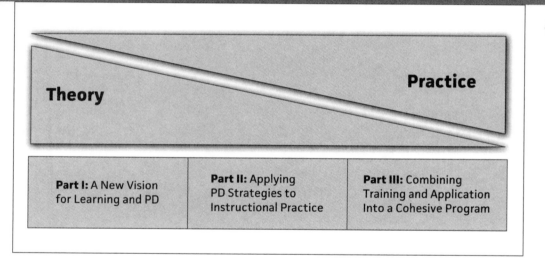

Theory		Practice
Part I: A New Vision for Learning and PD	**Part II:** Applying PD Strategies to Instructional Practice	**Part III:** Combining Training and Application Into a Cohesive Program

CHAPTER 3

● ● ● ● ● ● ● ● ● ● ● ● ● ● ● ● ● ●

Supporting Rigorous Learning for All

This chapter explores how to develop critical elements of a comprehensive professional development (PD) approach that incorporates instructional technology and maintains a focus on effective instruction. Focusing on the elements in this chapter will lead to a rigorous and personalized instructional program. The PD plan and tools introduced in the previous chapter play a significant role in enhancing blended learning instruction; we will review their impact in greater detail in this chapter. Consider Figure 3.1 on page 57 as you evaluate how your organization will incorporate these elements into one cohesive and impactful PD program. The PD program components listed include a reference to the chapters in which they are applied in detail. In this chapter, we will focus on rigorous learning for all, which includes

- Differentiated supports for equitable access
- Rigorous, constructivist learning opportunities
- Effective questioning to facilitate constructivist learning
- Student collaboration

As we review how these can be utilized to improve student learning, consider using Figure 3.1 to plan out your PD program for the school year. Revisit it often as you read through Part II to identify which focus areas to prioritize during different parts of the school year. There should be a methodical flow to the PD sessions based on your findings in the previous chapter and your specific organization's PD needs. The impact of the PD program will be maximized if monthly topics build on the previous ones and connect to the overall vision for PD established at beginning of the year. For example, topics can flow

Part I: A New Vision for Learning and Professional Development

---

Chapter 1: Elements of an Effective Blended Learning Classroom

- Effective instructional practices from distance learning
- Effective instructional practices from the traditional classroom
- A focus on conceptual understanding and constructivist learning

Which come from...

Chapter 2: Planning an Effective PD Program

- Peer observations in BL classrooms *(tips in Chapters 3 & 5)*
- PLCs focused on best practices *(tips in Chapters 3 & 4)*
- Tech integration with a focus on instruction *(tips in Chapters 3 & 4)*
- Research on BL theory and effective practices *(tips in Chapters 4 & 5)*
- Analysis of effective models in a BL classroom *(tips in Chapter 5)*
- Teacher workload sustainability *(tips in Chapter 5)*

That focuses on...

Part II: Applying PD Strategies to Instructional Practice

CH. 3: RIGOROUS LEARNING FOR ALL	CH. 4: PERSONALIZED ASSESSMENT & FEEDBACK	CH. 5: CLASSROOM CULTURE
• Differentiation for equitable access • Constructivist learning opportunities • Effective questioning • Student collaboration	• Assessments to gather actionable data • Actionable feedback for all students • Facilitating self-monitoring • Peer feedback	• Digital citizenship training • Learning environments in a BL model • A collaborative learning culture • Tech integration and management

And leads to...

Part III: Bringing Training and Application Together in One Cohesive Program

---

Conclusion: *Bringing It All Together*

- Creating a vision based on key takeaways
- Focused leadership during the transition
- Building your professional development team
- Collaborating with students and parents as stakeholders
- Soliciting feedback on distance learning
- Sharing blended learning impact on student learning
- Preparing students for a new world

FIGURE 3.1 ● Yearlong Professional Development Planner

	FOCUS AREA	JUSTIFICATION FOR THIS TIMELINE	HOW WILL YOU UTILIZE...					
			PEER OBSERVATIONS	PROFESSIONAL LEARNING COMMUNITIES	TECHNOLOGY INTEGRATION	RESEARCH	MODEL ANALYSIS	SUSTAINABILITY
August								
September								
October								
November								
December								
January								
February								
March								
April								
May								
June								
July								

Figure 3.1 is available as a downloadable template on the Companion Website at Resources.Corwin.com/BlendedLearningPlanner.

seamlessly from effective questioning to formative assessment data analysis to actionable feedback and finally to students in order to facilitate participants making connections and seeing how one topic informs the other. Addressing various skills in isolation will lessen the impact of each. We will revisit Figure 3.1 in the conclusion so you can refine your plan for the year.

DIFFERENTIATED SUPPORTS FOR EQUITABLE ACCESS

Arguably the most important benefit of utilizing blended learning is the ability to provide individualized differentiation to ensure all students are successful. This is particularly critical for at-risk students who need additional support. Review your organization's vision for PD in Figure 2.1 to inform your planning and guide your instructional expectations for all teachers. As you plan, emphasize the distinction between "teaching" and "learning." If the focus is on teaching, an effective lesson that reaches most students will be considered satisfactory because the lesson was *taught*, and whether students *learned* is secondary. However, if the focus is on *learning*, an effective lesson will not be enough; the teacher will need to check for understanding and provide differentiated support until he or she has evidence that *all* students have learned. Use Figure 3.2 to plan next steps using an inventory of PD supports utilized during distance learning. If limited examples are available, the leadership team must carefully examine how it will identify supports to inform PD planning.

BLENDED LEARNING FOR SOCIAL JUSTICE

As you recall your organization's vision for PD, assess how well it supports all students' learning, including those with limited access to resources and those who may need additional support. Establishing a vision that articulates a clear plan to differentiate and support all students' learning can be referenced time and again to maintain focus on serving all students. A vision that does not specify this may inadvertently allow some students to slip through the cracks.

FIGURE 3.2 ● Revisiting Your Professional Development Vision

Recall your school's or district's vision for professional development from Figure 2.1	
What professional development was provided to ensure differentiated instruction and equitable access during distance learning?	
What are some effective differentiation strategies that resulted from the training?	
How did students respond to these strategies?	
How will these efforts transfer to a blended learning setting?	
What additional supports will be necessary?	

 Figure 3.2 is available as a downloadable template on the Companion Website at Resources.Corwin.com/BlendedLearningPlanner.

Peer observations are a great way to identify effective approaches to differentiation. Start with the PD inventory in Figure 3.2 and build on these strategies in your PD plan. After differentiation strategies are discussed, schedule peer observations to see how instructional technology can be used to personalize learning for students. The observation protocol in Figure 3.3 can be used to look for differentiation in action.

FIGURE 3.3 ● Peer Observation Protocol for Differentiation

	CLASSROOM 1	CLASSROOM 2	CLASSROOM 3
Classroom Info (subject, grade, date, time)			
What data points does the instructor use to identify differing needs?			
Describe the differentiated activity: What are students doing?			
Describe the differentiated activity: What is the instructor doing?			
How is instructional technology used to facilitate differentiation?			
What differentiation trends do you observe for at-risk student subgroups?			

 Figure 3.3 is available as a downloadable template on the Companion Website at Resources.Corwin .com/BlendedLearningPlanner.

The observation findings should provide plenty of information to inform your organization's professional learning communities (PLCs). Identify best practices and trends with the findings and schedule regular meeting times to discuss next steps. Figure 3.4 can be used to facilitate the conversations.

FIGURE 3.4 ● Professional Learning Community Discussion Questions

How did differentiation impact learning in your observations? How do you know?	
What role, if any, did blended learning have in facilitating differentiation?	
What takeaways can you incorporate in your own classroom?	
What *technical* supports will you need to implement in your own classroom?	
What *instructional* supports will you need to implement in your own classroom?	
What action steps will you take to enhance differentiation in your classroom?	
How will you ensure that student learning has been impacted?	

 Figure 3.4 is available as a downloadable template on the Companion Website at Resources.Corwin.com/BlendedLearningPlanner.

These conversations in PLCs can inform PD topics and outcomes. By combining targeted peer observations and PLCs with the PD program, teachers will receive multi-pronged support both in and out of the classroom on how to differentiate learning to ensure all students succeed. Remember to keep the focus of PD on instruction, not technology or resources. Use instructional technology to enhance adult learning but leave technical directions for an optional session or follow-up to maintain the focus on learning. Consistent targeting of instructional practices coupled with technical support as part of a comprehensive PD plan throughout the year will dramatically improve classroom instruction while simultaneously improving instructional technology use, which in turn will prepare students for the rigorous expectations of constructivist learning.

Ideas for Professional Development Sessions

What follows are two scenarios used to show the distinction between focusing on technology and focusing on instruction:

1. Teacher sets up differentiated stations, and students self-select their station based on the amount of support they need.

2. Teacher administers a formative assessment and uses the data to inform small-group instruction.

In the first scenario, PD should focus on differentiated instructional techniques in small groups instead of on distributing and managing devices in stations.

In the second scenario, PD should focus on data analysis and actionable next steps instead of technical skills to develop a digital formative assessment.

RIGOROUS, CONSTRUCTIVIST LEARNING OPPORTUNITIES

One of the greatest benefits of blended learning is the ability to facilitate constructivist learning opportunities that engage students in rigorous learning through exploration and meaning making. Implementing blended learning with instructional technology does not automatically lead to constructivist learning, however. It must be explicitly introduced, and training must be provided to prepare teachers for constructivist learning design. Since constructivist learning requires a completely different approach to designing learning activities, a thorough understanding of the philosophy should be the focus of PD sessions on the topic.

Conducting and discussing research as part of professional learning described in the second chapter fits well with constructivist learning training. It fosters dialogue among educators on instructional philosophy, the potential benefits and drawbacks of constructivist learning, and its impact on lesson planning and student achievement. PD should consistently have applications to support learning but tying that work to research can increase buy-in and support understanding of non-traditional learning approach.

Technology integration is another important consideration when developing professional learning opportunities on constructivism. Students can make meaning by analyzing models, conducting research, and exploring different approaches, all of which can be enhanced by technology integration. These learning activities can have a tremendous impact on student learning, but their open-ended nature can also lead to lost instructional time if students lose focus of their learning goals. Pedagogical guardrails are critical for fostering intellectual curiosity and meaning making, while ensuring the efficient use of time and resources. Consider the parameters you will put in place to facilitate constructivist learning through technology and use Figure 3.5 to plan next steps with your team.

FIGURE 3.5 ● Planning for Constructivist Learning

How will you build teachers' capacity to be open to exploring constructivist learning as a framework for lesson planning?	
Where will you find research for your teaching teams?	
How will you connect research to concrete instructional practices to promote constructivist learning?	
How will you use instructional technology to promote constructivist learning?	
What are some examples of projects that give students opportunities to make meaning?	

 Figure 3.5 is available as a downloadable template on the Companion Website at Resources.Corwin.com/BlendedLearningPlanner.

Ideas for Professional Development Sessions

Create scenarios for each subject in which teachers pose questions that prompt research, analysis, and proposed solutions from students to topics that are aligned with standards. Students have a variety of choices on how to explain their findings. Discuss how this personalization enhances student understanding in each subject.

EFFECTIVE QUESTIONING TO FACILITATE CONSTRUCTIVIST LEARNING

Consider the type of prompts that will solicit constructivist learning. Questions that facilitate constructivist learning prompt inquiry, research, discussion, and analysis; they typically do not have single word or phrase answers. Your PD plan should include sessions on effective questioning, including the types of question prompts that solicit inquiry, rigorous discussion, and opportunities for students to demonstrate in a variety of ways based on how they make meaning. This last approach may receive professional pushback on the basis that "there is only one correct answer" in subjects such as mathematics. However, it is important to note that meaning making through constructivist learning does not advocate for accepting a variety of answers that may not be correct; rather, it suggests that students can use a variety of approaches to demonstrate mastery that heightens the learning experience. For example, a student can understand how to add fractions using visual aids, manipulatives, arithmetic steps, or other approaches, all of which lead to the correct conclusion. The *process* of learning how to apply those approaches to the problem—not the final answer—is where learning takes place. Instructional technology can greatly enhance this experience by offering more options for demonstrating mastery.

Incorporate guidance on how to develop prompts that facilitate constructivist learning in your PD plan. In subject area groups, teacher teams can collaboratively create learning opportunities driven by effective questioning. Recall from Figure 1.5

"Impact of Rigorous Prompts and High-Level Questioning" that rigorous learning opportunities must be coupled with effective questioning focused on constructivist learning to truly offer differentiated and collaborative learning.

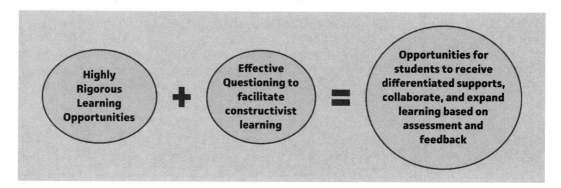

To assist in planning, work together to answer the questions posed in Figure 3.6.

FIGURE 3.6 ● Planning for Effective Questioning

How will you know if the prompts will foster constructive learning?	
How will you use instructional technology to facilitate constructivist learning using effective questioning?	
Describe the professional development needed to prepare teachers for implementation.	
What role will peer observations and professional learning communities play in implementing effective questioning?	
How will you measure success?	

 Figure 3.6 is available as a downloadable template on the Companion Website at Resources.Corwin.com/BlendedLearningPlanner.

STUDENT COLLABORATION

Another important instructional practice to target through PD is student collaboration. Collaboration on rigorous, constructivist learning activities fosters critical thinking and prepares students for success in their pursuits after graduation. Student collaboration aligns particularly well with blended learning as several tools that foster collaboration have been introduced in recent years. Students can work together on online documents to conduct research and build interactive presentations, and can use technology to connect with other students and content experts around the world. They can gather data, lead discussions, and share insights and findings with other students. The possibilities are limited only by access to technology and the design of learning opportunities they participate in.

TECH TIP

Be sure to establish security measures when setting up online collaboration resources. Collaboration documents should be shared specifically with the students who will have access to editing, and students must log in before they can collaborate. This increases security and also shows teachers each student's contributions to the process, which can inform next steps regarding supports needed. Before diving into online collaboration, be sure students have reviewed digital citizenship expectations, which are covered in more detail in Chapter 5.

Consider how you will utilize technology in classrooms and what PD supports will be necessary to prepare teachers for collaborative learning implementation. Since teachers were exposed to online interactions with students during distance learning, connecting training to their insights from distance learning may be a good place to start. Teachers can share their experiences facilitating student collaboration during distance learning to set a foundation to build on in a blended learning classroom. Use Figure 3.7 to gather an inventory of collaborative learning opportunities and plan for PD supports.

FIGURE 3.7 ● Fostering Student Collaboration

What opportunities did you create for students to learn collaboratively during distance learning?	
How was learning enhanced by these opportunities?	
What barriers did students have to overcome?	
How can this inform student collaboration in a blended learning setting?	
How will you balance in-person collaboration with online collaboration? When does it make sense to use each?	

 Figure 3.7 is available as a downloadable template on the Companion Website at Resources.Corwin.com/BlendedLearningPlanner.

Reflect on the responses and how they will inform PD on student collaboration. Consider sharing the examples below as you prepare your PD plan.

Key Takeaways

In this chapter, we reviewed how the critical elements of PD based on blended learning can support an effective instructional program, including

- Offering differentiated supports for equitable access for all students

- Developing rigorous, constructivist learning opportunities

- Utilizing effective questioning to facilitate constructivist learning

- Fostering student collaboration to enhance learning

The next chapter will apply the PD program to personalized assessment and feedback to effectively gauge student mastery levels, inform differentiation, and foster a culture of student self-monitoring.

CHAPTER 4

• • • • • • • • • • • • • • • • • •

Embracing Personalized Assessment and Feedback

This chapter explores how personalized assessment and feedback can inform differentiation instruction and planning, ultimately leading to student success. Without formative data, gaps in understanding will only be revealed in summative assessments near the end of the unit, which does not give the teacher enough time or information to support learning throughout the unit. Formative assessments and their analysis are essential in a blended learning classroom because they provide frequent and essential updates on student progress. The information we gather about student progress should inform the planning process and how we differentiate instruction. The chapter will examine how actionable feedback can enhance learning opportunities for all students, and how instructional technology can facilitate gathering and analyzing these data points. The main areas of focus will be

- Assessments to gather actionable data
- Actionable feedback for all students
- Facilitating self-monitoring
- Peer feedback

Part I: A New Vision for Learning and Professional Development

Chapter 1: Elements of an Effective Blended Learning Classroom

- Effective instructional practices from distance learning
- Effective instructional practices from the traditional classroom
- A focus on conceptual understanding and constructivist learning

Which come from...

Chapter 2: Planning an Effective PD Program

- Peer observations in BL classrooms *(tips in Chapters 3 & 5)*
- PLCs focused on best practices *(tips in Chapters 3 & 4)*
- Tech integration with a focus on instruction *(tips in Chapters 3 & 4)*
- Research on BL theory and effective practices *(tips in Chapters 4 & 5)*
- Analysis of effective models in a BL classroom *(tips in Chapter 5)*
- Teacher workload sustainability *(tips in Chapter 5)*

That focuses on...

Part II: Applying PD Strategies to Instructional Practice

CH. 3: RIGOROUS LEARNING FOR ALL	*CH. 4:* PERSONALIZED ASSESSMENT & FEEDBACK	*CH. 5:* CLASSROOM CULTURE
- Differentiation for equitable access - Constructivist learning opportunities - Effective questioning - Student collaboration	- Assessments to gather actionable data - Actionable feedback for all students - Facilitating self-monitoring - Peer feedback	- Digital citizenship training - Learning environments in a BL model - A collaborative learning culture - Tech integration and management

And leads to...

Part III: Bringing Training and Application Together in One Cohesive Program

Conclusion: Bringing It All Together

- Creating a vision based on key takeaways
- Focused leadership during the transition
- Building your professional development team
- Collaborating with students and parents as stakeholders
- Soliciting feedback on distance learning
- Sharing blended learning impact on student learning
- Preparing students for a new world

To understand the critical role of formative assessments, imagine that the teacher is going to lead a caravan of cars from Los Angeles to New York. Each student is driving one of the cars following the teacher. How often should the teacher look in the rearview mirror to see if all the cars are still following the lead car? If the teacher looks for the first time after driving through several states, the caravan will likely have lost some of the cars, and it will be immensely challenging and time-consuming to find exactly where they were each lost. The lead car may have to drive back through many states to find them. By regularly checking on the cars, however, the teacher can ensure the student cars are on the road and quickly provide support if one of them needs help with a tire change or mechanical failure. Similarly, formative assessments help the teacher check for understanding to get a sense of how well students are following along. If a student is struggling, the teacher can provide the support needed to help the student get back on the road. Formative assessments inform instructional practice and are among the most actionable data points in a teacher's pedagogical toolkit.

Before we proceed, it is important to note that the purpose of a formative assessment is to provide the teacher with information about student mastery and to inform next steps to help students toward it. When used effectively, formative assessments instill a growth mindset in students because students know the teacher is using the data points to determine how content that has not been mastered yet can be taught. If formative assessments are graded, they may lose some of this potency as the focus shifts from learning content not yet mastered to a consequence for not having mastered the content at that moment in time.

. . . .

Using formative assessments specifically to identify learning gaps sends the message to students that you are not satisfied with teaching and moving to the next topic; you will not have achieved your goal as a teacher until students learn.

. . . .

It is also important to note that "integrating formative assessment requires advance planning but can be done with small tweaks to an existing course and without increasing instructor workload. Flexibility is very important, as tweaks may be needed after implementation" (Kelley et al., 2019, p. 7). Thoughtful planning and implementation give teachers space to reflect on what they want to assess and what they will do with the findings.

ASSESSMENTS TO GATHER ACTIONABLE DATA

Most formative assessments fall in one of two categories: (1) those that provide general information about the entire class's mastery level; and (2) those that provide feedback on the skills and knowledge for individual students. The former can inform lesson pacing and differentiated prompts, while the latter is critical for developing intervention and enrichment opportunities. Both are essential for differentiated and targeted learning and both must successfully answer the same question: What type of actionable data will this formative assessment provide, and how will these data be used? Formative assessment use in a traditional classroom setting varies dramatically from classroom to classroom and this inconsistency persists in distance learning, suggesting an analysis of use in both settings is a good place to start. Use Figure 4.1 to gather an inventory of actionable formative assessment practices to inform PD planning.

Reflect on the responses and how they will inform PD on student in your professional learning communities (PLCs). The PLC should focus on the purpose of formative assessments and the importance of actionable data. Instead of revolving around various types of formative assessments, make next steps based on the data the center of the discussion. What do you want to know about student learning from your formative assessment? How did your formative assessment give you these actionable data? What are you planning to do next? Most importantly, emphasize that formative assessments have limited impact if the data points they produce are not reviewed and acted upon in a timely manner.

FIGURE 4.1 ● Actionable Formative Assessments

How did you gather formative data during in-person teaching?	
How did you gather formative data during distance learning?	
Did your use of the data differ between the two settings? If so, why?	
How did students respond in each instance?	
What purpose did the formative data serve?	
Which formative assessment approaches used during distance learning can effectively be used in the classroom?	
What are some ways you differentiated student learning experiences based on the formative assessment data?	
How can formative assessments inform constructivist learning opportunities?	
What are the advantages and disadvantages to collaborative formative assessments?	

 Figure 4.1 is available as a downloadable template on the Companion Website at Resources.Corwin .com/BlendedLearningPlanner.

Instructional technology can play a key role in analyzing the responses to a formative assessment and providing feedback quickly to students to maintain progress toward mastery. Where a short formative assessment on paper can take time to score and consolidate, the one using technology can generate individual and class data to inform next steps in a timely manner. Getting feedback to students shortly after the formative assessment dramatically increases the impact of the assessment as the data inform additional supports and review needed before progressing further.

Formative assessments have limited impact if the data points they produce are not reviewed and acted upon in a timely manner.

Formative data should be gathered frequently to gauge student understanding; a single formative assessment near the end of the lesson will be too little too late for students who needed support earlier in the lesson. Going back to the road trip analogy, that would be the same as checking to see how many cars are still in the caravan at the end of each day. Any car that didn't make it to the rest stop could be several hundred miles away. Frequent checks for understanding greatly increase the possibility of moving all students toward the learning objective. Once you have gathered data points from a formative assessment, you can use them to inform next steps.

As your team discusses the role of formative assessments in a blended learning setting, consider the difference between convergent and divergent assessments:

> convergent types of formative assessment typically accept or elicit knowledge that strictly aligns with the

teacher's expectations, which creates inequities in the classroom by pushing students' nuanced strategies to the background. Instead, teachers who move toward divergent formative assessments welcome disagreement, confusion, and mistakes as a part of the learning process. (Kalinec-Craig, 2017, p. 4)

Divergent formative assessments align with constructivist learning practices, facilitate inquiry and meaning-making, and fit well in a blended learning program. Teachers should frequently utilize divergent formative assessments to gauge understanding, as well as further promote rigorous learning opportunities. Be mindful of the type of responses you receive from the formative assessments. Students may demonstrate understanding in many ways and developing formative assessments that capture this feedback in many ways can give teachers more accurate information about what students understand and where they need additional support. Some formative assessments may be convergent, but opportunities for students to articulate their mastery level in a variety of ways should be incorporated into lessons to inform planning and next steps.

BLENDED LEARNING FOR SOCIAL JUSTICE

As you develop formative assessments using instructional technology to get timely feedback, ensure that you are using a divergent format that elicits inquiry. Convergent assessments based on one particular expectation may put some student groups at a disadvantage. Prompting all students to demonstrate understanding by making meaning in line with their background offers a more equitable approach.

ACTIONABLE FEEDBACK FOR ALL STUDENTS

As mentioned in the previous section, formative assessments provide data points on the class' mastery level or individual students' progress depending on how they are set up. For formative assessments that involve polling or anonymous surveys, for example, provide class-level data points. The teacher uses this information to see if a concept should be reviewed again, taught using a different approach, or explored further in small groups. How helpful formative data points become depends largely on how well they are designed from the outset. An effective formative assessment gives the teacher a wealth of information, while taking up the least amount of time. To do this, every question must have a purpose, a reason for being included in the assessment. The teacher should ask, "How will this question directly impact what I do next?" Maximizing impact comes from gleaning information about student understanding from incorrect answers as well. Thoughtful questions reveal details about student understanding, even if a student chose an incorrect answer. For example, if students are asked to add 1/4 and 3/4 consider that incorrect answers will reveal misconceptions. In this case, students choosing 1/2 as an answer show that they are adding both the numerator and denominator to get 4/8. Reflect on the incorrect answer choices you can include to identify misconceptions such as this. If the correct answer is 1, avoid simply listing 0, 1, 2, 3, and 4 as answer choices. Once you have this information, be sure to use a constructivist learning approach to ensure students discover why we do not add denominators. Telling them that it is a rule will not be effective long term; instead, use visuals, manipulatives, digital resources, or higher-order questioning to help students make meaning of why the numerators are added and to internalize the justification. Give them an opportunity to explain their reasoning to their peers.

This is also a great opportunity to apply PD around effective blended learning practices that facilitate small-group instruction. If only a small group of students need additional support based on formative assessment data, the classroom can quickly convert to a station model that creates space for small-group instruction. Students review content with the teacher, while other students apply their learning in collaborative projects designed to enhance understanding. Teachers who decide to use this approach should develop consistent routines on using a station model to minimize the time required to switch from whole-group instruction. In the next chapter, we will look more closely at classroom procedures to facilitate differentiation and blended learning models. Formative assessment data can also be used to facilitate student self-monitoring, which we will explore later in this chapter.

Ideas for Professional Development Sessions

Have PD participants experience the transition from whole group to differentiated small groups themselves to better understand what it looks like in the classroom. Pose a question and show what grouping can look like. Create a second opportunity to transition and compare to the first.

To bring these elements together into one cohesive process, let's look at an example from beginning to end. In this scenario, a teacher can lead instruction in one of three ways:

1) Whole-group direct instruction

2) Small-group direct instruction in a rotation model

3) Flipped classroom with videotaped lesson followed by live discussion

In all three approaches, the teacher checks for understanding with formative assessments using a combination of technology-based and traditional tools. Based on the results, the teacher can take a variety of next steps:

1) If the formative data points reveal broad misconceptions or gaps in understanding, the teacher revisits the approach and addresses the issue for the class. The teacher considers different learning modalities and considers students' conceptual understanding to ensure they internalize the learning.

2) If the majority of the class demonstrates understanding, the teachers provide them with collaborative learning opportunities using technology to apply what they have learned to more rigorous prompts. During this time, the teacher pulls small groups of students based on the formative data to provide review and intervention as needed. The teacher can pull different small groups to address different areas as the formative data necessitates. A clear process to quickly forming small groups should be in place to minimize transition time. Technical resources are available to students to provide support while the teacher is working with the smaller group.

TECH TIP

The teacher should have several technical supports in place that can answer questions while the teacher is working with students in small groups. Some examples include

- Login information page that students can reference for support on how to access various online programs used in class
- Video screencasts with steps on how to use collaborative apps such as the google suite for education
- Assigned "tech team" students who can provide support with technical issues
- Online FAQ page where students can submit questions the teacher can answer after concluding small-group instruction

While approaches to address formative assessment data will vary from classroom to classroom, highlighting its importance and effectiveness should be a critical part of your PD plan. In addition to utilizing PLCs to discuss effective approaches to formative assessment and actionable data analysis, consider introducing the concept of *common formative assessments* (CFAs) to enhance student learning. By developing CFAs collaboratively as a team, checks for understanding can be used across classrooms, leading to broader conversations about best practices. Teachers have data that can be used to plan next steps with formative assessments, but common formative assessments also give teachers potential next steps on how to address the data. If, for example, students struggled to answer a particular formative assessment prompt in one class but students in another teacher's class successfully responded to the prompt, the teachers can discuss approaches used to see why one seemed to be more effective than the other. This type of collaboration not only facilitates these types of critical discussions, it also sparks conversation on what topics should be prioritized and why. To foster this culture of collaboration, be sure to schedule opportunities for teaching teams to come together to explore CFAs.

TECH TIP

Technology dramatically aids teachers in developing common formative assessments and maximizes their collaboration time. Multiple teachers can add questions/prompts to a collaborative document in preparation for collaboration time. They can also co-develop formative assessments using sites such as google forms and illuminate.

To determine the most appropriate differentiated supports for formative assessment training in your PD plan, consider using formative data with your teaching team. One option is to offer a survey in advance on formative assessment use and instructional technology expertise to inform your planning. Another is to allow teachers to self-select their PD group based on their experience and need. Using these data points, create a differentiated PD learning experience. Figure 4.2 is an example of what the experience can look like.

FIGURE 4.2 ● Example of Differentiated Professional Development on Formative Assessments

	FOR TEACHERS WITH LIMITED EXPERIENCE CREATING FORMATIVE ASSESSMENTS AND/OR UTILIZING THE DATA FOR PLANNING	FOR TEACHERS PROFICIENT WITH FORMATIVE ASSESSMENTS IN A *TRADITIONAL CLASSROOM SETTING*	FOR TEACHERS PROFICIENT WITH FORMATIVE ASSESSMENTS IN A *DISTANCE LEARNING SETTING*	FOR TEACHERS PROFICIENT WITH FORMATIVE ASSESSMENTS IN A *BLENDED LEARNING SETTING*
Who can lead this group?				
What instructional technology prerequisites are needed?				
How will you check for understanding?				
How will divergent formative assessments be incorporated to facilitate constructivist thinking?				
What next steps should the group plan for?				

 Figure 4.2 is available as a downloadable template on the Companion Website at Resources.Corwin .com/BlendedLearningPlanner.

For each group, consider presenting research articles to high-light the importance of formative assessments and how they can be used in distance, blended, and traditional classroom settings. In addition to sparking intellectual curiosity, research articles can help start conversations about formative assessment philosophies and how they impact student achievement. Some questions to guide discussion include the following:

- How does the implementation and impact of various formative assessments differ in various instructional settings?

- How do you measure the effectiveness of formative assessments in each setting?

- How do you determine the appropriate timing and frequency of formative assessments?

Use this opportunity to also model differentiation and the different ways you can plan for the groups. PD session leaders can gather data on participants' expertise to form groups, or they can ask participants to self-select their groups which requires self-monitoring, an approach we will explore in the next section. Regardless of approach, be sure to explicitly call out how you differentiated the groups before the end of the session and allow time for participants to reflect on how they can apply the differentiation strategy in their own classrooms. This can also become a focus area for the PLCs targeting formative assessment and data analysis.

FACILITATING SELF-MONITORING

One of the best indicators that students are taking ownership of their learning and that teachers have established a growth mindset culture in their classroom is when students begin to effectively self-monitor their learning. In an effective blended learning setting, a "teacher's role is not to direct student learning but to support students to self-direct learning and to facilitate active student engagement in learning through strategies such as self-monitoring and self-evaluation" (Wehmeyer et al., 2017, p. 297). In classrooms where learning, not grades, are emphasized and students know the goals they are working toward and why they are learning, they know what they know and know what they still need to learn. In a classroom where students self-monitor, an observer can ask students what they are working on, and they can articulate what they have learned and what they are still working on mastering. In this type of learning environment with self-monitoring, formative assessments provide data on progress not just to the teacher, but also to the students.

DISTANCE VS. BLENDED LEARNING

Students can also self-monitor in a distance learning setting, but the blended learning classroom offers opportunities to share their progress in stations based on students' self-assessments. Create space for students to discuss their progress in a constructive way and establish a classroom culture that reinforces the notion that everyone is working together toward the same goals.

It takes training and practice to develop this type of culture in the classroom. As part of the formative assessment sessions in your PD plan, consider incorporating training for implementing self-monitoring. Use Figure 4.3 to inform your planning.

· ·

In a learning environment built around student self-monitoring, formative assessments provide data on progress not just to the teacher, but also to the students.

· ·

As you discuss the potential impact of self-monitoring on student learning, consider what resources you can provide to facilitate the development of this skill. A few options that can support this work include the following:

- *Self-reflection protocols:* Students regularly respond to prompts about what they learned, what they still need to learn, and what next steps they will take.

- *Self-assessment rubrics:* For learning activities that will be assessed using a rubric, create space for students to first self-assess and score their work using the rubric. Students should provide explanations for their scores

FIGURE 4.3 ● Incorporating Self-Monitoring Training

How did students self-monitor progress toward mastery during distance learning? Does this approach carry over into a blended learning setting?	
How will students benefit from self-monitoring progress toward mastery?	
What role will instructional technology play in facilitating student self-monitoring?	
How will your self-monitoring protocol facilitate students' understanding of their own learning?	

 Figure 4.3 is available as a downloadable template on the Companion Website at Resources.Corwin/BlendedLearningPlanner

and special recognition can be given to students whose self-assessment matches the teacher's rubric results, indicating that the student is demonstrating a high level of self-monitoring. Note however, that "a rubric guides a student in the process of self-assessment, although it does not provide feedback by itself. Rubrics for self-assessment help students to ask relevant questions about their inquiry process . . ." (Psycharis, 2016, p. 324).

- *Self-monitoring charts:* Teachers can provide self-monitoring charts for students to keep track of their learning. These charts should be designed to show growth and increased rigor over time instead of simply being presented as a checklist of standards students are working toward learning. The self-monitoring chart should be designed in conjunction with the course curriculum plan to maximize alignment and focus. If the course is designed from the outset to rapidly teach and check off standards instead of guiding students through a rigorous, holistic, and constructivist learning experience, the self-monitoring chart will reflect that planning decision. Review the self-monitoring charts in your PD sessions to see how well they reflect the type of learning environment you want to see in all classrooms. They can also lead to power conversations about pedagogical philosophy in your PLCs.

TECH TIP

Consider developing a digital self-monitoring chart using a spreadsheet program such as Microsoft Excel or Google Sheets that students can use to record and manage their progress toward mastery. Students can gather both qualitative and quantitative data on progress, and learn how to apply formulas and develop visual presentations to show their growth. This experience also helps them develop analytical skillsets that will be critical both in college and future careers.

PEER FEEDBACK

Finally, consider incorporating peer feedback as part of the PD sessions on formative assessment. As teachers progressively learn about more formative assessment approaches, some can begin exploring how students can advance constructivist learning by creating opportunities for peer feedback. Peer feedback protocols create space for students to share their understanding with their classmates, get feedback, and pose questions to heighten learning. This also gives students a chance to share their approach to a prompt and compare it to others' responses to see how others "made meaning," ultimately leading to deeper connections with the content and more internalized learning. Seeing other peers' perspectives or proposed solutions gives students multiple angles through which to view the prompt. Opportunities for peer feedback lead to constructivist thinking as students discuss their findings in small groups and reach conclusions together.

Consider using a model that borrows some elements from a traditional dissertation defense. Students are given a rigorous prompt to explore and draw conclusions. They conduct research, analyze findings, and make meaning. They then present their findings to their peers in small groups and answer questions about their presentation. Students can use a questioning protocol to facilitate the conversation. This process offers several benefits:

- Students individually or collaboratively utilize instructional technology to explore a topic and apply constructivist thinking to the prompt

- Students self-assess before presenting in a small group

- Students who are uncomfortable presenting can record their presentation for viewing before answering questions

- Peers practice active listening during the presentation and during the questions

- Presenters practice writing, speaking, listening, and researching throughout the process

Review the formative assessment implementation options in Figure 4.4 and start a conversation about your organization's current level and readiness for enhancements that can further inform instruction and increase students' growth mindset.

FIGURE 4.4 ● Formative Assessment Implementation Options

	WHO ASSESSES UNDERSTANDING? WHO PROVIDES FEEDBACK?	IMPACT ON DEEPER UNDERSTANDING	ROLE OF INSTRUCTIONAL TECHNOLOGY	IS YOUR ORGANIZATION READY FOR THIS APPROACH? HOW DO YOU KNOW?
Teacher-administered formative assessments in a blended learning setting	Teacher	Teacher identifies students' strengths and learning gaps and develops differentiated supports to ensure all students succeed.	Teacher can manage and aggregate results quickly using quizzes, surveys, polling software, or student electronic submissions.	
Formative data through self-monitoring	Teacher and student (Teacher provides feedback on student self-assessment.)	Self-monitoring helps students to better understand their own learning gaps and work toward mastery, enhancing growth mindset. Teacher provides feedback on both the reflection process and the content.	Students can show their progress toward mastery by using digital tools.	
Formative data through peer feedback	Teacher and students (Students provide feedback to each other after self-assessment and teacher provides feedback on their findings.)	In addition to growth mindset development through self-monitoring, students better understand how their peers made meaning of the content, enhancing constructivist learning. Teacher provides feedback on both the reflection process and the content.	Collaborative online documents can be used to collect feedback, add comments, and pose questions.	

Figure 4.4 is available as a downloadable template on the Companion Website at Resources.Corwin/BlendedLearningPlanner

Key Takeaways

In this chapter we reviewed how formative assessments and data analysis can inform instruction and planning as well as reinforce students' growth mindset. The impact of formative assessments can be enhanced by student-centric learning opportunities, including

- Self-monitoring progress

- Providing peer feedback

With effective PD, teachers can incorporate these strategies into their blended learning classrooms to facilitate constructivist and differentiated learning. In Chapter 5, we will explore the blended learning classroom environment required to effectively incorporate the instructional approaches from Chapter 3 and the formative assessment approaches from this chapter.

CHAPTER 5

• • • • • • • • • • • • • • • • •

Creating a Blended Learning Culture

This chapter will explore the training needed to establish a classroom culture and logistical layout conducive to utilizing instructional technology. Effective, differentiated learning is the ultimate goal in the classroom, so beginning with that end in mind can help us plan our classroom culture better. This chapter will cover some logistical considerations for setting up a classroom environment that supports blended learning, but the main focus will be on establishing a classroom culture that fosters collaboration, encourages innovation and exploration, and personalizes learning to ensure all students get the support they need to succeed.

The importance of planning cannot be overemphasized when planning learning activities for students. Anticipate challenges and create solutions; establish supports; and set clear expectations for collaboration, transitions, and self-monitoring. Thoughtful planning takes time but has several advantages:

- It allows teachers to focus on instruction and learning instead of being pulled away to address logistical or technical concerns.

- It allows teachers to take on a facilitator role in the classroom, guiding students to take ownership of their learning and self-monitor.

Part I: A New Vision for Learning and Professional Development

Chapter 1: Elements of an Effective Blended Learning Classroom

- Effective instructional practices from distance learning
- Effective instructional practices from the traditional classroom
- A focus on conceptual understanding and constructivist learning

Which come from...

Chapter 2: Planning an Effective PD Program

- Peer observations in BL classrooms *(tips in Chapters 3 & 5)*
- PLCs focused on best practices *(tips in Chapters 3 & 4)*
- Tech integration with a focus on instruction *(tips in Chapters 3 & 4)*
- Research on BL theory and effective practices *(tips in Chapters 4 & 5)*
- Analysis of effective models in a BL classroom *(tips in Chapter 5)*
- Teacher workload sustainability *(tips in Chapter 5)*

That focuses on...

Part II: Applying PD Strategies to Instructional Practice

CH. 3: RIGOROUS LEARNING FOR ALL	CH. 4: PERSONALIZED ASSESSMENT & FEEDBACK	CH. 5: CLASSROOM CULTURE
• Differentiation for equitable access • Constructivist learning opportunities • Effective questioning • Student collaboration	• Assessments to gather actionable data • Actionable feedback for all students • Facilitating self-monitoring • Peer feedback	• Digital citizenship training • Learning environments in a BL model • A collaborative learning culture • Tech integration and management

And leads to...

Part III: Bringing Training and Application Together in One Cohesive Program

Conclusion: Bringing It All Together

- Creating a vision based on key takeaways
- Focused leadership during the transition
- Building your professional development team
- Collaborating with students and parents as stakeholders
- Soliciting feedback on distance learning
- Sharing blended learning impact on student learning
- Preparing students for a new world

- It fosters sustainability as teachers have less of a need to run from group to group to address issues, which also maximizes instructional time with students not having to wait as long for teacher support.

The table below once again highlights our areas of focus and where they fall in the professional development (PD) plan. This chapter will show how peer observations, research on blended learning theory and models, and strategies for sustainability can be used in your PD program to establish a collaborative and constructivist learning environment. Specific topics addressed include:

- Digital citizenship training

- Learning environments in a blended learning model

- Establishing a collaborative learning culture in classrooms

- Technology integration and management

THE RISE OF DIGITAL CITIZENSHIP TRAINING

As more of our experiences move online, digital citizenship has become more critical than ever. Digital citizenship is no longer an optional topic of focus for schools and districts that are using instructional technology; it is essential for anyone who uses online platforms, social media, or learning apps. Even if your organization prioritized digital citizenship during distance learning, reviewing its core tenets for the blended learning classroom is essential. Not only does digital citizenship reinforce the importance of positive behavior, but it establishes norms that are crucial for collaboration, discussion, peer feedback, and other learning activities discussed so far. Without clear expectations on digital citizenship, the classroom is not ready for those types of rigorous learning opportunities.

As you consider how digital citizenship training will be implemented, note that establishing digital citizenship expectations based largely on teacher oversight will quickly lead to frustration and exhaustion as teachers spend increasingly more time monitoring student behavior online, while limiting students' positive connections with the teacher. Teachers will not be able to keep up with the constant monitoring, and even more time will be spent reacting to infractions and limiting access to online sites and experiences as a consequence, which will create the need for planning alternative learning activities. Instead, make expectations clear and develop opportunities for students to internalize the importance of positive behavior both online and in the classroom. Review case studies with them and ask them to reflect on their own experiences interacting with others online. Students will need to remember digital citizenship expectations long after they graduate and can be held accountable by teachers and administrators; if we want students to be prepared for their future careers and relationships, internalizing positive online behavior is paramount.

TECH TIP

There are many reputable sites that offer free digital citizenship training for schools and districts to use. One of the most highly regarded sites is *Common Sense Media*, which offers free digital citizenship training curriculum including lessons and videos. The curriculum is age specific and broken down by topic. Classroom posters are also available.

As you create your plan for digital citizenship PD, reflect on your distance learning experience and how digital citizenship expectations might shift between distance and blended settings. Use Figure 5.1 to start the conversation.

FIGURE 5.1 ● Planning for Digital Citizenship Training

How did your team communicate digital citizenship expectations during distance learning?	
How can you assess the effectiveness of that training?	
In what ways will digital citizenship expectations need to be updated in a blended learning classroom?	
How, if at all, are digital citizenship expectations different than traditional classroom expectations?	
What expectations can the team commit to upholding across classrooms?	
What type of supports will teachers need to effectively train students on digital citizenship expectations?	

 Figure 5.1 is available as a downloadable template on the Companion Website at Resources.Corwin .com/BlendedLearningPlanner.

As with any expectation established for the classroom, successful implementation is dependent on clarity, consistency, and revisiting as necessary. Training students on digital citizenship expectations at the beginning of the school year and moving forward without revisiting them may not be successful. Model digital citizenship expectations and look at various scenarios to apply them. At least one example should be on a collaborative learning opportunity and how teams work together and share responsibilities. A scenario addressing conflicts is also important to include. Consider examples that address

- Differing opinions on a controversial topic

- Challenges within the team on a collaborative project

- Sharing personal information online

- Cyberbullying

Peer observations are a great way for teachers to see effective digital citizenship expectations in action. Observers can examine how

- Students demonstrate positive communication and collaboration at various stations when the teacher is at another station.

- Students interact and collaborate with each other both in person and online.

- Digital citizenship expectations are shared and reinforced in different blended learning models.

- Students use instructional technology as a resource for learning, not as an opportunity to harm each other or themselves.

- The observation protocol in Figure 3.3 can be used to look for differentiation in action.

You can use Figure 5.2 to guide peer observations for digital citizenship.

FIGURE 5.2 ● Peer Observation Protocol for Digital Citizenship

	CLASSROOM 1	CLASSROOM 2	CLASSROOM 3
Classroom Info (subject, grade, date, time)			
Evidence of positive interactions between students in-person			
Evidence of positive interactions between students online			
How are citizenship expectations communicated?			
How are students held accountable for behavior?			
How does the blended learning model use reinforce digital citizenship?			

 Figure 5.2 is available as a downloadable template on the Companion Website at Resources.Corwin .com/BlendedLearningPlanner.

LEARNING ENVIRONMENTS IN A BLENDED LEARNING MODEL

Digital citizenship is a key prerequisite of an effective blended learning classroom environment, but there are logistical considerations as well. How a classroom is set up can dramatically impact student learning, as well as sustainability. Marquez et al.

(2016) conclude that "classroom management training is both a cognitive and a behavioral process that needs to be carefully aligned with teacher needs" (p. 103). Indeed, careful planning must be used when considering how students will

- Transition to different activities
- Rotate from one station to the next
- Get technical support
- Get differentiated instructional support

It is important to distinguish between personalization and differentiation: "Personalization gives students some control over the instructional decisions, while differentiation indicated that the teacher or software is making all the decisions" (Graham et al., 2019, p. 249). Learning opportunities can be personalized to give students choices on how to approach the topic to best fit their learning modality, but the classroom environment must have clear directions for differentiated supports. If systems are not in place for students to experience differentiated learning based on formative assessments, self-monitoring protocols, and other data points, the teacher will spend excessive time guiding students to the supports they will need. This in turn will lead to limited opportunities to lead small-group instruction and challenges with sustainability as the teacher becomes in-demand by multiple students with different needs at one time.

Also consider how routines can impact instruction, both in terms of learning and in terms of time saved during transition. Shin et al.'s (2018) research demonstrates that consistency in students' seating position can have an impact on learning. When students rotate between stations or learning opportunities, going to the same seat creates consistency and allows students to focus more on the assignment. These authors describe three different types of seating options with the settler demonstrating the highest achievement:

- "The Settler: Sits at the same position more than 14 times
- The Semi-nomad: Sits in a 3-by-3 range or in the same row or the same column more than 14 times
- The Nomad: Sits at a random position"

Classroom layout and seating position consistency were not considerations during distance learning but will need to be discussed to maximize learning in each classroom. Share research and start a conversation with your team on how these logistical issues can set up students for success.

Ideas for Professional Development Sessions

Discuss the layout of the PD learning space:

- Do teachers consistently sit in the same area each week?
- When is sitting in another part of the room conducive to learning?
- When does moving negatively impact learning?

Have a conversation about the impact of the learning space and seating, especially in a blended learning classroom with stations and no traditional "front" of the classroom.

Another important topic to discuss with your team is sustainability: How will teachers meet the demands of differentiated learning at multiple stations in a timely manner without burning out? A critical strategy is to anticipate challenges and to develop solutions for students to access. Minimizing the need to pause instruction to tend to logistical concerns can help teachers focus on student mastery and help them learn to take ownership of their learning. Parkinson et al. (2013) emphasize the need to "Empower students in both distance learning and traditional settings to take more ownership for their own learning. This includes knowing how to interrupt and signal the instructor when problems arise, especially ones related to technology, such as poor visibility and audio difficulties." As much as possible, give students opportunities to own their learning by allowing them to research solutions to challenges, share their expertise with others, and demonstrate mastery. A technical cheat sheet with login information and how-to guides described earlier is essential.

As much as possible, give students opportunities to own their learning by allowing them to research solutions to challenges, share their expertise with others, and demonstrate mastery.

Making resources available is not enough. This also requires a mindset shift in the concept of the teacher as the purveyor of knowledge. Traditionally, students learned from the teacher but with the teacher now in the new role of a facilitator, they form a variety of sources carefully curated and planned by the teacher. If students ask a question that the teacher cannot answer, the teacher can encourage students to find more information on the topic and share the findings. Now that we have unlimited access to information, it will not be uncommon for teachers not to have all the answers. Encouraging research and analysis fosters the constructivist learning process all blended learning classrooms should embrace.

TECH TIP

Examples of logistical support teachers can provide to assist with sustainability include

- Creating login help pages that show students how to access frequently used sites if they cannot remember their login credentials. These can be online or on flyers around the room with QR codes that students can scan to access the information

- Creating or locating how-to videos for using instructional technology resources such as collaborative google apps, reading programs, and research sites

To further aid sustainability, teacher teams can share the load of creating these resources. They can create a collaborative document and split up the responsibility of adding videos and links. Another benefit of this approach is that students will experience consistency in accessing technical support from classroom to classroom.

Use Figure 5.3 to brainstorm logistical challenges students and teachers faced during distance learning and how they can be addressed in the blended learning classroom.

FIGURE 5.3 ● Addressing Logistical Challenges

What types of challenges did students face during distance learning with accessing instructional sites and getting directions on how to use instructional technology resources?	
How did they access solutions to these challenges during distance learning?	
Which of these solutions, if any, can transfer to a blended learning classroom environment?	
How will the team make these solutions accessible to students in every classroom?	

 Figure 5.3 is available as a downloadable template on the Companion Website at Resources.Corwin.com/BlendedLearningPlanner.

DISTANCE VS. BLENDED LEARNING

Carefully review resources used in distance learning and determine which ones can be utilized in a blended learning classroom to aid in sustainability. Look specifically for screencasts, how-to sites, and templates you used. Many can transfer to a blended learning classroom.

ESTABLISHING A COLLABORATIVE LEARNING CULTURE IN CLASSROOMS

Once classroom learning environments are established with thoughtful layouts, readily available supports accessible to students, and digital citizenship training, we can begin exploring how student collaboration can significantly enhance student learning and engagement. Student collaboration is an essential component of the constructivist learning experience because the discussions and interactions students have facilitate critical thinking and inform each student's own meaning-making about the topic. Singh et al. (2019) conclude, "allowing more flexibility in engaging with the course material, and creating a more positive atmosphere in which they built off of each other's learning, [leads] to significant improvements in exam performance" (p. 303). Student collaboration may be considered by some a novel learning approach that has benefits but ultimately takes too much time, but be assured that it is a crucial component of the blended learning experience. Collaboration must be incorporated both in-person and online to build on each other and ultimately create a more rigorous and robust learning experience for all students.

Take, for example, a lesson on important figures during World War II. In a blended learning setting, students can choose a figure, conduct research, create an interactive learning experience for their peers, self-assess using a rubric, and solicit feedback and questions from other students using an established protocol. For this project, they must draw their own conclusions about the impact the figure had on the outcome of the war and if they would have approached things differently. The learning experience promotes constructivist thinking and includes personalization through choice, meaning-making based on students' reflection, peer feedback, and self-monitoring. Now imagine the same learning opportunity with additional opportunities for collaboration. Two students can choose their figures and explore how the actions of one impacted the other. They can discuss historical events from the perspective of their figures and determine how their figures' actions impacted others. By learning more about the impact on others, they can develop a deeper understanding of their figure's own actions, which in turn can inform their conclusions about their figure. With this added collaborative component, students now have opportunities to extend their thinking further and draw more layered and insightful conclusions.

These collaborative learning opportunities can be incorporated into any blended learning model, but careful planning is necessary to set students up for success. Adjustments to how prompts are presented, supports provided, and learning outcomes achieved may be required depending on the model used. In a station rotation model, for example, students can receive direct instruction in one station before moving to another to conduct research, and another for discussion and collaboration. In contrast, students in a flipped-classroom model can conduct research at home and come to school with information and analysis ready for collaboration. The learning objectives are the same, but the format and directions are slightly different. Jdaitawi (2019) explains, "Flipped classrooms also facilitate students' collaboration to explore novel ideas and knowledge concerning the subject under study" (p. 674). Students are also able to continue working together at home using collaboration documents such as Google Docs or Slides.

TECHNOLOGY INTEGRATION AND MANAGEMENT

One of the most frequently voiced frustrations during distance learning was the challenge students and teachers faced with technical issues such as slow Internet connections, difficulty accessing content, and online security issues. Some of these issues will persist in a blended learning classroom and can impact students' learning, but there are others to consider as well. Technical issues can derail a lesson, and transition time lost accessing technology and managing hardware can take away from precious instructional time. Thoughtful planning on logistics, training students, and not relying solely on technology for learning can effectively maximize learning in a blended learning classroom. In this section, we will explore best practices for technology integration and management and the planning involved to ensure success. According to Laiken et al. (2014), "It takes much longer to develop blended learning than a classroom experience ... material needs to be thoroughly tested to ensure the concepts are clear, and the technology works as planned" (p. 302).

First, remember that instructional technology is just one of many resources available to teachers to create engaging and rigorous learning experiences for students. Should technology become unavailable, learning does not need to stop. The teacher, not the technology, is the ultimate facilitator of learning. To that end, make sure all teachers have backup plans in case the Internet goes down, technology becomes unavailable, or other issues arise. Use your responses in Figure 5.3 to inform your planning.

Second, establish clear protocols for accessing and returning devices in the classroom. This need did not exist during distance learning, and students will need specific training on when, where, and how to access devices in class. Emphasize again that technology is a resource, not the learning outcome and that resources must be used to enhance learning. They will not need technology for all learning and only need to access devices when the learning opportunity calls for it. Students can still use books, pencils, and paper.

TECH TIP

There are several approaches to managing technology in the classroom. If students will go to a charging cart to access a computing device, consider allowing students to go to the cart after they complete a "Do Now" learning activity when they enter the classroom. Instructions for next steps can be waiting for them on your site.

Another helpful technology management strategy that also empowers students involves creating and using a tech team in your classroom. Students are digital natives—they have been familiar with computers from an early age—and can lead support teams to assist their peers as needed. Teachers can empower them as tech experts to take on leadership roles in the classroom and support each other's learning. They can even contribute to a growing library of how-to screencasts located in one place to expand their impact. The success of the tech team depends on how teachers introduce the concept, encourage involvement, and show appreciation. It is a respected role and one that must be taken seriously by participants. Consider giving the team a name that connects to the school's vision or mascot and celebrates their contributions.

Be sure to offer a training program to maximize the effectiveness of the tech team. The training should be teaching strategies to help other students, not on technical skills. This "mini-credential" approach has been successful in our district in preparing students for peer tutor roles. Focus areas include asking questions to better understand students' struggles, ensuring that students learn by doing instead of watching, and identifying ways to check for understanding. Be sure to include recommendations on how to connect with various learning modalities to make sure all students are successful; auditory, visual, and other learning styles should be accommodated. The tech team can also pursue opportunities to explore advanced technologies, which can ultimately lead to learning applications in the classroom. Examples include green screen technology to record video presentations and three-dimensional printing to bring designs to life.

BLENDED LEARNING FOR SOCIAL JUSTICE

Our commitment to ensuring the success of *all* students means students in schools serving communities of a low socioeconomic status must be given the same opportunities as their peers in more affluent areas. Access to more advanced hardware is a critical step toward achieving this goal. Fortunately, many organizations have identified this need and offer grants that include both hardware and training. Often, these grants are available specifically to Title I schools. Identify a team in your organization to find and apply for these grants. It will be well worth the effort.

Another important decision regarding tech integration and management is choosing a learning management system (LMS) that will store lessons and other learning materials, facilitate the submission and return of assignments, create space for online discussion, and organize content. Some popular LMS programs are Blackboard, Canvas, Moodle, and Google Classroom. Each offers a different layout and has varying advantages and disadvantages, but they all serve to help teachers manage students' learning. Having an LMS also allows students to easily access content they want to revisit or lessons they may have missed due to illness. Educators rightfully advocate for using the LMS that best serves their students' needs, and impassioned conversations can be expected over which one is better. As much as possible, try to reach consensus on one LMS for your organization for two reasons:

- Consistency between classrooms will lead to fewer logistical issues for students that can get in the way of accessing content and take attention away from learning.
- The information technology department will be able to respond faster to technical issues that impact learning with fewer programs that serve the same purpose.

Some districts consider using two LMS platforms: one that is more user-friendly for younger students, and a more robust option for older students.

TECH TIP

In addition to adopting an LMS, determine whether there is a need for a single sign-on app to help students manage their programs and logins. One popular option is clever, which integrates with Google apps for education and allows students to access several instructional programs with one username and password.

Finally, consider the impact of allowing students to take devices home. To ensure equitable access to technology both at school and at home, schools may need to consider providing computing devices and wireless hotspots for students to take home. With ever-shrinking budgets, this is not a small task. However, students who have no access to a device at home can potentially take one of the classroom computing devices to help minimize the need for additional hardware purchases. Several companies will offer affordable insurance plans in case of damage to minimize loss. Schools can explore purchasing Internet hotspots for students who do not have online access at home. Some districts have already purchased these hotspots in case of online access required out on sports fields and other outdoor locations; these devices can be utilized to minimize expense. While these device purchases may be viewed as outside the scope of schools' responsibilities, it is our collective mandate as educators to ensure all students succeed as instructional technology is becoming an increasingly critical component of students' learning and preparation for the careers of the future. For this reason, we must do everything in our power to ensure students have access to the tools they need to be successful.

Key Takeaways

In this chapter, we explored how to establish a classroom culture and layout that facilitates blended learning, including

- Fostering digital citizenship
- Creating collaborative learning opportunities for all students
- Addressing logistical and technical challenges
- Empowering students to take on leadership roles in the classroom

In the final chapter, we will integrate the approach described in Part I with the practical applications detailed in Part II to create one cohesive PD program.

Bringing Together Training and Application Into One Cohesive Program

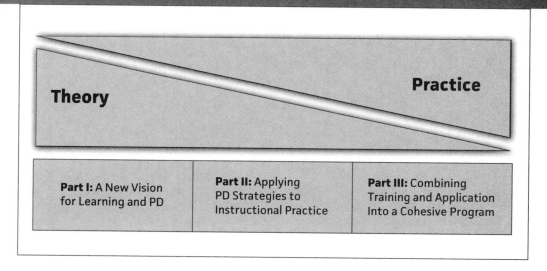

Theory

Practice

Part I: A New Vision for Learning and PD	**Part II:** Applying PD Strategies to Instructional Practice	**Part III:** Combining Training and Application Into a Cohesive Program

CONCLUSION

● ● ● ● ● ● ● ● ● ● ● ● ● ● ● ● ● ● ●

Bringing It All Together

The first five chapters of this book explored the process of incorporating the best of distance learning to a blended learning classroom, enhancing learning through collaboration and constructivist learning, and developing professional development (PD) opportunities to prepare your teams for implementation. Your team has used the figures throughout this book to facilitate discussion around these ideas and begin planning PD modules. With so many moving parts required to work together to build coherence around these ideas, we must step back, look at the overall plan, and see how it all comes together. In this final chapter, we will draw from the previous chapters to assemble a plan ready for implementation. We will also explore when and how the plan can be implemented and how to prepare stakeholders for a transition during an already uncertain time.

CREATING A VISION BASED ON THE KEY TAKEAWAYS

As we consider how to integrate the concepts described in this book into a practical plan for implementation, it's important to review the key takeaways from the first five chapters:

CHAPTER 1: HOW WILL SCHOOLS TRANSITION BACK TO THE CLASSROOM?

- Instructional practices from the distance learning experience can supplement effective teaching in a traditional classroom environment to inform a successful blended learning program.

- Blended learning can enhance conceptual understanding and constructivist learning to increase rigor and offer differentiated supports to ensure all students succeed.

- A collaborative approach to reflection and planning will facilitate the successful implementation of your organization's blended learning program.

CHAPTER 2: RETHINKING PROFESSIONAL DEVELOPMENT IN BLENDED LEARNING

- The shift from distance to blended learning requires a unique vision for PD and includes

  o Peer observations in blended learning classrooms

  o Professional learning communities focused on best practices

  o Technology integration, including a focus on instruction

  o Research on blended learning theory and effective practices

  o Detailed analysis of effective models in a blended learning classroom

  o Understanding how to develop strategies and resources to ensure sustainability of the lesson planning workload and continuous direct instruction in some station models

- PD must maintain a sustained focus on instruction, not resources.

- Growth opportunities for educators must be prevalent to foster professional learning.

CHAPTER 3: SUPPORTING RIGOROUS LEARNING FOR ALL

- Critical elements of blended-learning-based PD can support an effective instructional program, including

  o Offering differentiated supports for equitable access for all students

- Developing rigorous, constructivist learning opportunities
- Utilizing effective questioning to facilitate constructivist learning
- Fostering student collaboration to enhance learning

CHAPTER 4: EMBRACING PERSONALIZED ASSESSMENT AND FEEDBACK

- We reviewed how formative assessments and data analysis can inform instruction and planning, as well as reinforce the students' growth mindset. The impact of formative assessments can be enhanced by student-centric learning opportunities, including

  - Self-monitoring progress
  - Providing peer feedback

CHAPTER 5: CREATING A BLENDED LEARNING CULTURE

We explored how to establish a classroom culture and layout that facilitates blended learning, including

- Fostering digital citizenship

- Creating collaborative learning opportunities for all students

- Addressing logistical and technical challenges

- Empowering students to take on leadership roles in the classroom

Each of these topics contributes to a professional learning plan that

- Is grounded in research

- Leverages and builds on the skills and knowledge generated from the distance learning experience

- Prioritizes constructivist thinking and collaborative learning

- Applies PD strategies to the following three main focus areas:

  o Instructional practice in a blended learning setting
  o Formative assessments and next steps informed by results
  o Classroom culture and management

The conversations your team has had and the questions you answered as you read this book should give you a strong sense of how to proceed. You may refer to your responses to the prompts in the previous chapters to build your PD plan. The flowchart at the start of the chapters in Part II is shown again with the final development step included and a listing of where each chapter fits in the planning process. As mentioned at the start of the second chapter, the PD plan should be co-designed and co-led by teachers to include their voice and expertise in the process. For many schools, this shift to more prominently incorporating instructional technology into the school plan will be a dramatic change, and making it teacher driven will dramatically impact its effectiveness and reception.

FOCUSED LEADERSHIP DURING THE TRANSITION

The transition to blended learning comes after a period of unprecedented uncertainty in our institutions as safety concerns forced educators to rethink how they teach, assess, and plan in new environments and with new expectations. As schools reopen and begin reflecting on the distance learning experience and how it will shape the future, they will need their leadership teams to take on two seemingly conflicting roles:

- Providing stability and consistency to guide the transition back to in-classroom instruction and campus life

- Generating innovation and inspiration to expand the effectiveness of the current program by introducing blended learning and instructional technology from the distance learning experience

Part I: A New Vision for Learning and Professional Development

---

Chapter 1: Elements of an Effective Blended Learning Classroom

- Effective instructional practices from distance learning
- Effective instructional practices from the traditional classroom
- A focus on conceptual understanding and constructivist learning

Which come from...

Chapter 2: Planning an Effective PD Program

- Peer observations in BL classrooms *(tips in Chapters 3 & 5)*
- PLCs focused on best practices *(tips in Chapters 3 & 4)*
- Tech integration with a focus on instruction *(tips in Chapters 3 & 4)*
- Research on BL theory and effective practices *(tips in Chapters 4 & 5)*
- Analysis of effective models in a BL classroom *(tips in Chapter 5)*
- Teacher workload sustainability *(tips in Chapter 5)*

That focuses on...

Part II: Applying PD Strategies to Instructional Practice

CH. 3: RIGOROUS LEARNING FOR ALL	*CH. 4:* PERSONALIZED ASSESSMENT & FEEDBACK	*CH. 5:* CLASSROOM CULTURE
• Differentiation for equitable access • Constructivist learning opportunities • Effective questioning • Student collaboration	• Assessments to gather actionable data • Actionable feedback for all students • Facilitating self-monitoring • Peer feedback	• Digital citizenship training • Learning environments in a BL model • A collaborative learning culture • Tech integration and management

And leads to...

Part III: Bringing Training and Application Together in One Cohesive Program

Conclusion: *Bringing It All Together*

- Creating a vision based on key takeaways
- Focused leadership during the transition
- Building your professional development team
- Collaborating with students and parents as stakeholders
- Soliciting feedback on distance learning
- Sharing blended learning impact on student learning
- Preparing students for a new world

Balancing the consistency piece with innovation will not be easy, requiring nuance, good timing, reflection, and buy-in from multiple stakeholder groups. Focusing too heavily on stability and consistency will lead schools right back to their programs before distance learning, which is not an ideal outcome, regardless of the historic success of the organization. Updates to existing programs to maximize student learning must be done consistently: as educators, we are lifelong learners and must learn from the distance learning experience. Though the pandemic had devastating consequences, we must find the silver lining of this tragic chapter for the sake of our students and use this opportunity to revisit practices, reflect on our impact, and introduce new resources and approaches to learning to ensure the success of all students. To revert right back to the status quo suggests that we were content with all aspects of our instructional program before the pandemic, and that is good enough for our students; for struggling students—and every organization has them—this is a disservice.

Conversely, focusing too heavily on innovation during the transition can have detrimental consequences as well. During distance learning, students, parents, teachers, and administrators all experienced schooling in a completely new format and the change was both sudden and forced; they crave the normalcy of classroom instruction, in-person interaction, and activities that became severely limited, such as sports and the arts. They must be given opportunities to reconnect with their school community and previous experiences.

DISTANCE VS. BLENDED LEARNING

The shift to distance learning was unexpected and immediate, forcing educators to transition to an innovative new approach to instruction as the only way to continue student learning. Blended learning, however, should not be forced on educators upon return to the classroom. Unlike the unexpected transition to distance learning, it requires exploration, discussion, and an extensive training program. Expect more success after you garner buy-in and develop your training program collaboratively. The blended learning approach requires a considerable investment in time and effort, and a quick implementation may not yield the desired outcome.

To balance these important needs of your school community, you must carefully plan the approach and timing of the blended learning PD plan to maximize its impact. A critical step in this process is to be transparent about your intentions and the vision that drives your leadership team. Share the plan to incorporate instructional technology and a constructivist thinking approach to classroom instruction, and explain the benefits. Cite research, including references made in this book, to support your plan and reiterate the importance of using the distance learning experience as a learning opportunity to further impact student success. Emphasize that this transition will ultimately give students rigorous opportunities that prepare them for the careers of tomorrow and that it is itself enough to warrant consideration. Also, be sure to stress that this transition will be planned and implemented collaboratively with teacher input and that it does not impact content standards.

Most importantly, speak from the heart and inspire your team to support this transition, because it is best for students. While no instructional approach is without flaws, the blended learning approach combines many of the best practices of in-person and distance instruction to differentiate and personalize learning, while nurturing the relationships critical for establishing connections with students; it is the right thing to do for our students. Furthermore, the gaping difference between the constructivist and personalized learning experiences of students in many affluent schools that prepare them for leadership roles and the more traditional learning experiences of students in under-resourced schools must be eliminated. All students, regardless of their school, must have access to opportunities for rigorous, collaborative, and differentiated learning. For this reason, the transition to blended learning is all the more critical for schools in communities with a low socioeconomic status.

Consider the questions in Figure 6.1 as you plan your vision and PD program. They provide an opportunity to discuss how you will implement the PD plan you will design later in the chapter and who you will collaborate with to maximize the effectiveness of the training sessions. The first question is of particular importance as it asks leaders to reflect on how they will simultaneously manage the dual responsibilities of steady leadership during uncertain times and spearheading an innovative initiative that will lead to organizational change.

The organizations that best find this balance will be the most successful when they return from distance learning.

These are challenging questions, and some may not have readily available answers, but anticipating them and reflecting on what the answers reveal about your readiness for implementation will inform your success. Keep in mind that you do not need to wait for all conditions to be perfect for implementation; make sure the critical players who will support the PD plan are ready, and begin the process.

FIGURE 6.1 ● Final Steps Before Rolling Out Your Plan

How will you provide steady leadership during the transition while promoting an innovative professional development plan?	
Who are critical faculty members and administrators who can help build support around the professional development plan?	
Who are critical faculty members and administrators who can co-plan and co-lead the professional development plan?	
How do you anticipate the blended learning professional development plan to be received?	
How will you determine when you have enough support to proceed?	
How will you address pushback from faculty members or administrators on the timing of implementation?	
What additional supports do you need for successful implementation? How will you get this support?	

 Figure 6.1 is available as a downloadable template on the Companion Website at Resources.Corwin.com/BlendedLearningPlanner.

BUILDING YOUR PROFESSIONAL DEVELOPMENT TEAM

Your PD team selection is essential for the success of the program. Find teachers who have a passion for instruction and pedagogical research and have conversations about their experiences both in the classroom and in the distance learning setting. Identify areas of expertise they can share with others, and determine which PD topics they can co-develop and co-lead. Ideally, you will be able to identify at least one educator for each focus area at the start of the year and schedule planning time with them in advance. The school year can be hectic, especially one after the transition back from distance learning, so reaching out to collaborators shortly before the PD date may not yield the best results. Set your vision, identify your PD plan focus areas based on your organization's experience, and schedule planning opportunities with your team for the year. During each planning session, be sure to reflect on the previous session and build on that experience to create connections and context, which will in turn maximize the effectiveness of that session.

Once your team is ready, complete the prompts from Figure 6.2 using your discussions and responses in the tables throughout the first five chapters to develop your organization's blended learning PD plan. You may not be able to complete all the details for the

FIGURE 6.2 ● Blended Learning Professional Development Plan

Step 1: What is your school's or district's current vision for professional development?
(Refer to Figure 2.1.)
Step 2: What takeaways from the distance learning experience will you incorporate into this vision? (Refer to Figures 1.2 and 2.2.)

 Figure 6.2 is available as a downloadable template on the Companion Website at Resources.Corwin.com/BlendedLearningPlanner.

plan at the beginning of the year, but establishing the vision for PD from the outset is critical, as is identifying the focus areas and stakeholders who will share their expertise in those sessions.

Step 1: Refer to Figure 2.1 and write down your school's or district's vision for PD.

Step 2: Review your responses in Figures 1.2 and 2.2, and list which takeaways from the distance learning experience you will incorporate in your vision.

Step 3: Review your PD calendar in Figure 3.1. Determine when you will focus on each of the topics from Part II below and add them to the calendar. The sequence of topics that follows is provided as one possible approach that can be adjusted based on your organization's needs and prior experience and initiatives.

Chapter 3

- o Differentiated supports for equitable access
- o Rigorous, constructivist learning opportunities
- o Effective questioning to facilitate constructivist learning
- o Student collaboration

Chapter 4

- o Assessments to gather actionable data
- o Actionable feedback for all students
- o Facilitating self-monitoring
- o Peer feedback

Chapter 5

- o Digital citizenship training
- o Learning environments in a blended learning model
- o Establishing a collaborative learning culture in classrooms
- o Technology integration and management

YEARLONG PROFESSIONAL DEVELOPMENT PLANNER

	FOCUS AREA	JUSTIFICATION FOR THIS TIMELINE	HOW WILL YOU UTILIZE . . .						
			PEER OBSERVATIONS	PROFESSIONAL LEARNING COMMUNITIES	TECHNOLOGY INTEGRATION	RESEARCH	MODEL ANALYSIS	SUSTAINABILITY
August								
September								
October								
November								
December								
January								
February								
March								
April								
May								
June								
July								

Step 4: Add additional planning information to each month's topic, including

- What takeaways from distance learning will be applied to each topic

- Who can lead PD on this topic (if possible, plan to co-plan and co-lead with an administrator and at least one teacher)

- Identify how each will foster collaborative learning (refer to Figure 2.2)

- Identify how each will foster constructivist thinking (refer to Figure 2.2)

Before you complete the "Takeaways From Distance Learning to Apply" column, read the upcoming section titled "Collaborating With Students and Parents as Stakeholders" to include their perspectives on strategies that were effective during distance learning.

Step 5: Determine how you will check for understanding and how you will monitor progress toward the established mission and vision. Finally, determine baseline information before the training and your intended outcome for each topic.

Step 6: Once the PD plan layout draft is finalized, create hyperlinks to each PD training and add them to the document to establish a "one-stop-shop" for stakeholders. Connecting the trainings together offers several benefits, including

- Simplifying access for further discussion and regular reviews

- Serving as a check to ensure the PD training plans are aligned to the overall plan and vision

- Facilitating a collaborative approach to PD design

- Fostering a sense of transparency

- Challenging participants to make further connections and contribute to the development of upcoming training sessions

The PD plan will not be perfect. No training plan ever is. For this reason, it is important to continue refining and updating the plan as a "living document" in which edits and updates can be made to improve it. If the vision established in the first step is carefully developed with stakeholders and backed by the instructional team, these adjustments will be minor tweaks informed by outcome data. A vision for PD that does not meet these requirements may require an overhaul. The vision will also need to be shared with parents and students.

COLLABORATING WITH STUDENTS AND PARENTS AS STAKEHOLDERS

The shift to blended learning will dramatically impact students, that is, how they learn, what the classroom will look like for them, and what types of support they will receive. The research clearly shows its positive impact on student learning, and its essential role in closing the achievement gap, but parents will also need opportunities to understand better why the school is adopting it. In addition, students and parents will need to learn more about what to expect and how blended learning compares to distance learning and in-person instruction. There are three important aspects to student and parent involvement in the blended learning PD program:

- Soliciting their feedback on their experience during distance learning, which will inform Step 4

- Explaining how blended learning will positively impact student learning and prepare students for success

- Sharing what blended learning is and is not

SOLICITING FEEDBACK ON DISTANCE LEARNING

Throughout this book, we have reflected on the distance learning experience and how it prepared us for the transition to blended learning. In addition to gathering feedback from teachers on their distance learning teaching experience and how it can inform instructional technology use for blended learning, we must also solicit feedback from students and parents. Students' feedback is particularly critical as they are very insightful about what effective instruction looks like. Be sure to include their voices along with teachers' feedback to determine distance learning practices to include in Step 4. You can hold feedback sessions to capture student voices or can develop differentiated surveys for elementary, middle, and high schools to gather feedback. Prompts to consider are presented in Figure 6.3. You may also consider collecting quantitative data using Likert scales, but be sure to prioritize open-ended questions to get a clear sense of students' experiences.

FIGURE 6.3 ● Survey Prompts to Gather Student Feedback on Distance Learning

What is your grade level?	
Which school do you attend?	
What activities given by your teacher helped you learn the most during distance learning?	
What type of activities did you need the most help with?	
How did you get help when you needed it?	
Describe your experience working with other students online.	
What type of training do you wish you received more to prepare you for distance learning?	
Did you learn better with distance learning or when you were learning in the classroom? Why?	
What are some aspects of using computers for learning that you would like to continue using in the classroom?	
Which educational computer programs or apps helped you learn the most? Why?	
Describe how you worked with other students on learning projects during distance learning.	
What computer skills do you have that you can help your classmates with?	
What recommendation would you give to your teacher about using computers in the classroom?	

 Figure 6.3 is available as a downloadable template on the Companion Website at Resources.Corwin .com/BlendedLearningPlanner.

Any student survey designed to gather information on distance learning should be specific to your organization's distance learning experience, but these prompts can be used to start conversations about what information you want to gather. Survey questions can be customized to gather feedback from parents as well, especially for younger students. Be sure each question offers actionable data to inform PD planning.

TECH TIP

Consider using a survey app like Google Forms or Survey Monkey for your survey to simplify the aggregation of results as much as possible and ensure timely analysis. Be sure to include multiple languages to maximize access. Consolidating several versions of the survey in different languages can be cumbersome; instead, list each prompt in multiple languages if possible, to expedite analysis and avoid the need for lengthy consolidation.

SHARING THE IMPACT OF BLENDED LEARNING ON STUDENT LEARNING

Be sure to create opportunities for parents and students to learning more about blended learning and what the transition from distance learning will look like. Very few parents will have extensive knowledge about blended learning, especially since they did not experience it firsthand as students. Giving parents opportunities to learn more will help to make them allies, and their buy-in will ultimately improve student learning further. There are several ways to share information about blended learning:

- Information sessions, especially ones connected to popular school events to maximize attendance

- Webinars introducing blended learning (be sure to record the session and make it available online for later viewing)

- Regularly scheduled update sessions which include a Q&A portion

- Classroom observation opportunities so parents can see blended learning and instructional technology use in action

- Case studies to demonstrate how blended learning impacts lesson plans (see Figure 1.3)

. . . .

Giving parents opportunities to learn more will help to make them allies, and their buy-in will ultimately improve student learning further.

. . . .

The information sessions should include clear distinctions between traditional instruction and blended learning instruction. This not only includes the incorporation of instructional technology in the classroom, but also the pedagogical approach to lesson design. Blended learning incorporates discovery and meaning-making into the learning process, meaning not all information required is provided by the teacher; this stands in stark contrast to some students' past experiences in which a teacher provides all the information necessary, and students are asked to emulate it. Without clarifying these expectations, students may think that the teacher is insufficiently teaching the content when the teacher is intentionally creating opportunities for exploration, discussion, collaboration, and extension.

SHARING WHAT BLENDED LEARNING IS AND IS NOT

Parents will have many questions about blended learning, and they will get answers either from you or from other sources; providing answers up front will give parents clear answers and minimize the need to clarify misunderstandings later. One of the most common concerns over blended learning expressed by parents revolves around the role of instructional technology in classrooms. It is not uncommon to hear parents share that students learn better from their teachers than from computers and that computers will dramatically hamper students' socioemotional well-being due to reduced interaction with their peers. While an ineffective classroom runs the risk of validating these concerns, a well-designed and implemented blended learning program does quite the opposite.

First, computing devices are not meant to replace teacher instruction; instead, they enhance it by offering visuals, exploratory opportunities, and innovative approaches to reach multiple learning modalities. The teacher is still the designer of the lesson and continues to use direct instruction but does so in different formats to meet student needs. The teacher may regularly use small-group instruction based on differentiated needs, while students work on other learning opportunities designed by the teacher, for example.

Second, effective blended learning dramatically enhances student collaboration as they work together both online and in-person. Effective blended learning classrooms do not look like computer labs with students working quietly on their own; instead, students work in small groups, collaborating on projects, asking questions, rotating to stations, and sharing presentations. Not every student is on a computer at any given time; some are using computers, while others are having a discussion or receiving direct instruction from the teacher in a small group. The blended learning classroom is alive and includes movement, conversation, and camaraderie. It is a space in which students learn to interact positively with their peers both in person and online. It is also an environment in which students can express themselves in a variety of ways and using different resources. Parents who are not familiar with blended learning will need to better understand the expectations of the classroom and how it will impact students' socioemotional well-being.

BLENDED LEARNING FOR SOCIAL JUSTICE

Parents with a low socioeconomic status may have limited access to technology, which can impact their understanding of blended learning. Take the time to discuss terminology and language to help all parents get acclimated with instructional technology and become more comfortable accessing programs and supporting students at home.

PREPARING STUDENTS
FOR A NEW WORLD

As you lay the groundwork for your organization's blended learning program, keep in mind that your students are the first cohort in history to go from mandatory distance learning to blended learning. Pandemics have occurred in the past, but this is the first to occur since the advent of the Internet to facilitate collaborative learning from home. The sudden, unplanned shift forced stakeholders to embrace technology and rethink how they teach and learn; it is reasonable to conclude that after such a dramatic and prolonged departure from traditional learning environments, some of the lessons learned in distance learning will resonate for many years in classrooms globally. With the inevitable impact of expanded technology use by teachers, students, and parents, it is more important now than ever to learn from this experience and prepare our educators for effective instructional technology use in the classroom. No one knows what the classroom of the future will look like and how technology will impact how we learn, but collaborative learning and constructivist thinking will always be essential tenets of effective, differentiated instruction. Incorporating instructional technology in classrooms after distance learning without extensive training can lead to concerning scenarios:

- Instruction continues using the distance learning approach, which did not consistently offer constructivist and collaborative learning opportunities due to the circumstances of the rollout.

- Instruction reverts to traditional classroom approaches, limiting the use of instructional technology to differentiate learning.

- Instruction is limited by technical and logistical challenges with instructional technology, negatively impacting learning.

To maximize the benefits of instructional technology, we must not wait long to design and implement a blended learning PD plan. Training must begin shortly after students and teachers return to the classroom to immediately maximize learning.

Over time, instructional technology used without effective blended learning training can result in the challenges listed above. If your team is not ready to implement PD on blended learning, begin having the conversations about your vision upon return from distance learning and identify key stakeholders to connect with to begin this work.

* *

No one knows what the classroom of the future will look like and how technology will impact how we learn, but collaborative learning and constructivist thinking will always be essential tenets of effective, differentiated instruction.

* *

Blended learning helps bring these ideas to life in the classroom with proper training, and the promise of personalized, rigorous learning it offers should excite educators. Like with any new initiative, a lot of work needs to be done to achieve effective implementation, and adding this responsibility to exhausted educators may not seem like a great idea. Implementing an effective training program for instructional technology, however, is an investment in the future of our students and our schools. As educators, we have an ethical obligation to do right, and that includes keeping students safe and preparing them for the future; the blended learning PD program does both. It keeps students safe by training them on digital citizenship and appropriate uses of technology, which is becoming more prevalent in their lives each day. It also prepares them for the opportunities of the future by showing how technology can be used to address challenges, collaborate with others, locate and use data, draw conclusions, and much more. The opportunities of the future will not be the same as those of the past, and no one can perfectly predict what they will look like; we can, however, give students the critical skills they need to be prepared for whatever the future holds.

Our commitment to social justice also compels us to prepare students for success to close the achievement gap. Two critical elements of blended learning—constructivist thinking and technological proficiency—directly impact this discrepancy. Many schools in affluent neighborhoods are already embracing a constructivist approach to learning that fosters creative problem-solving, rigorous analysis, and research; limiting these opportunities for students in less affluent communities to focus solely on learning gaps taught in traditional formats without differentiation further widens the achievement gap. In that scenario, only one group of students is preparing for leadership and innovation. The same impact occurs if there is a disparity in student experiences with technology. The impact of technology on future opportunities is undeniable, and limiting technology use to working on specific apps effectively threatens students' success. We owe it to all students to offer learning experiences that maximize the resources we have, and that requires implementing an effective blended learning PD program.

Let's revisit the road trip analogy from Chapter 4, used to describe the impact of formative assessments. In that analogy, we saw that failing to check frequently whether students are successful and providing differentiated supports could lead to drivers getting lost along the trip. With instructional technology and blended learning dramatically expanding the rigor and depth of learning opportunities and offering extensive opportunities for exploration, the cars are driving at a much faster rate; more ground is covered each day on the journey. This means formative assessments are more important now than ever to ensure students are moving toward the learning goals. It also suggests that teachers need to provide additional support to students whose cars may need special support to perform well. As organizational leaders, you are charged with training the lead drivers to use effective strategies and check progress to make sure all cars make it to the end goal. Use this PD program to train your team and get them excited about starting this journey. Any new journey brings some apprehension, but this is a hopeful one that fosters engagement and intrigue. Remind everyone why we are taking this journey and why we chose to lead these teams.

Educators are deeply invested in instilling a love of learning in students and seeing them succeed. These goals will remain unchanged after the pandemic. Distance learning may have altered the format for instruction, but the goals remain the same as they do in a blended learning classroom. Now teachers have a powerful combination of instructional strategies and resources to further enhance their efforts and help more students succeed through differentiation. As you lead your teams toward developing the skills and experience required for effective instruction using constructivist thinking and collaborative learning, remember that we are also learners and must continue exploring the capabilities and applications of instructional technology and blended learning. Internet-based instructional technology that facilitates collaboration and research has been around for a tiny fraction of educational history, and even the most knowledgeable expert still has much to learn about this ever-evolving approach. Acknowledge that we all have more to learn and continue researching the topic. Recognize and celebrate the contributions of other teachers to the PD program and foster the notion that we are all lifelong learners. The pandemic altered many of our instructional plans and forced us to think critically about how we teach, assess, and manage. From the challenges of that distance learning experience, we will rise, grow, and become stronger.

References

Beckem, J. M., II, & Watkins, M. (2012). Bringing life to learning: Immersive experiential learning simulations for online and blended courses. *Journal of Asynchronous Learning Networks, 16*(5), 61–70.

Bonk, C. J., & Graham, C. R. (2004). *Handbook of blended learning: Global perspectives, local designs.* San Francisco, CA: Pfeiffer Publishing.

Corwin Herring, M. (2004). Development of constructivist-based distance learning environments: A knowledge base for K–12 teachers. *The Quarterly Review of Distance Education, 5*(4), 231–242.

Cronjé, J. C. (2010). Using Hofstede's cultural dimensions to interpret cross-cultural blended teaching and learning. *Computers & Education, 56*(3), 596–603.

Davis, N., & Rose, R. (2007). *Research committee issues brief: Professional development for virtual schooling and online learning.* Retrieved from http://www.inacol.org/wp-content/uploads/2012/11/NACOL_PDforVSandOlnLrng.pdf.

Graham, C., Borup, J., Pulham, E., & Larsen, R. (2019). K–12 blended teaching readiness: Model and instrument development. *Journal of Research on Technology in Education, 51*(3), 239–258.

Hammond, Z. (2014). *Culturally responsive teaching and the brain promoting authentic engagement and rigor among culturally and linguistically diverse students.* Thousand Oaks, CA: Corwin.

Harris-Packer, J., & Ségol, G. (2015). An empirical evaluation of distance learning's effectiveness in the K–12 setting. *American Journal of Distance Education, 29*(1), 4–17.

Herold, B. (2014). Private schools exploring blended learning models. Retrieved from http://www.edweek.org/ew/articles/2014/01/29/19el-private.h33.html.

Innosight Institute. (2012). *Classifying K–12 blended learning.* Lexington, MA: Author.

Jdaitawi, M. (2019). The effect of flipped classroom strategy on students learning outcomes. *International Journal of Instruction, 12*(3), 665–680.

Kalinec-Craig, C. (2017). The rights of the learner a framework for promoting equity through formative assessment in mathematics education. *Democracy & Education, 25*(2), 1–11.

Kelley, K. W., Fowlin, J. M. Tawfik, A. A., & Anderson, M. C. (2019). The role of using formative assessments in problem-based learning: A health sciences education perspective. *Interdisciplinary Journal of Problem-Based Learning, 13*(2), 1–11.

Knewton blended learning infographic. (2014). Retrieved from http://www.knewton.com/blended-learning/

Laiken, M., Milland, R., & Wagner, J. (2014). Capturing the magic of classroom training in blended learning. *Open Praxis, 6*(3), 295–304.

Ling, S., Ariffin, S., Rahman, S., & Lai, K. (2010). Diversity in education using blended learning in Sarawak. *US–China Education Review, 7*(2), 83–88.

Mac Mahon, B., Ó Grádaigh, S., & Ni Ghuidhir, S. (2019). Super vision: The role of remote observation in the professional learning of student teachers and novice placement tutors. *TechTrends, 63*, 703–710.

Marquez, B., Vincent, C., Marquez, J., & Pennefather, J. (2016). Opportunities and challenges in training elementary school teachers in classroom management: Initial results from classroom management in action, an online professional development program. *Journal of Technology and Teacher Education, 24*(1), 87–109.

Milthorpe, N., Clarke, R., Fletcher, L., Moore, R., & Stark, H. (2018). Blended English: Technology-enhanced teaching and learning in English literary studies. *Arts & Humanities in Higher Education, 17*(3), 345–365.

National standards for quality online teaching. (2011). Retrieved from http://www.inacol.org/wp-content/uploads/2013/02/iNACOL_TeachingStandardsv2.pdf.

Owston, R., & York, D. (2012). Evaluation of blended learning courses in the faculty of liberal arts and professional studies and the faculty of health—Winter session 2012. Technical Report No. 2012–3 (pp. 1–32). Institute for Research on Learning Technologies.

Parkinson, D., Greene, W., Kim, Y., & Marioni, J. (2003). Emerging themes of student satisfaction in a traditional course and a blended distance course. *TechTrends, 47*(4), 22–28.

Pregot, M. V. (2013). The case for blended instruction: Is it a proven better way to teach? *US–China Education Review, 3*(5), 320–324.

Preston, C. (2020). Coronavirus is the practice run for schools. But soon comes climate change. *The Hechinger Report.* Retrieved from https://hechingerreport.org/coronavirus-is-the-practice-run-for-schools-but-soon-comes-climate-change/.

Psycharis, S. (2016). The impact of computational experiment and formative assessment in inquiry-based teaching and learning approach in STEM education. *Journal of Science Education and Technology, 25,* 316–325.

Shin, Y., Junghyuk, P., & Lee, S. (2018). Improving the integrated experience of in-class activities and fine-grained data collection for analysis in a blended learning class. *Interactive Learning Environments, 26*(5), 597–612.

Singh, A., Rocke, S., Poorasingh, A., & Ramlal, C. (2019). Improving student engagement in teaching electric machines through blended learning. *IIEE Transactions on Education, 62*(4), 297–304.

Singh, H. (2003). Building effective blended learning programs. *Educational Technology, 43*(6), 51–54.

Ültanır, E. (2012). An epistemological glance at the constructivist approach: Constructivist learning in Dewey, Piaget, and Montessori. *International Journal of Instruction, 5*(2), 195–212.

Wehmeyer, M., Shogren, K., Toste, J., & Mahal, S. (2017). Self-determined learning to motivate struggling learners in reading and writing. *Intervention in School and Clinic, 52*(5), 295–303.

Yilmaz, K. (2008). Constructivism: Its theoretical underpinnings, variations, and implications for classroom instruction. *Educational Horizons, 86*(3), 161–172.

Index

Confident Teachers, Inspired Learners

CAROL PELLETIER RADFORD

This vivid and inspirational guide offers educators practical strategies to promote their well-being and balance. Readers will find wisdom for a fulfilling career in education through teachers' stories of resilience, tips for mindful living, and podcast interviews with inspiring teachers and leaders.

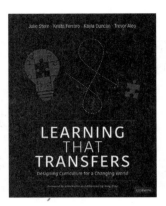

JULIE STERN, KRISTA FERRARO, KAYLA DUNCAN, TREVOR ALEO

This step-by-step guide walks educators through the process of identifying curricular goals, establishing assessment targets, and planning curriculum and instruction that facilitates the transfer of learning to new and challenging situations.

STEPAN MEKHITARIAN

Transition back to school by leveraging the best of distance learning and classroom instruction. Learn how to create a blended learning experience that fosters learning, collaboration, and engagement.

SHIRLEY CLARKE

Learning intentions and success criteria expert Shirley Clarke shows how to phrase learning intentions for students, create success criteria to match, and adapt and implement them across disciplines.

To order your copies, visit corwin.com